Theories of Truth.
An Introduction

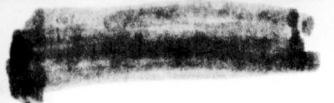

ALSO AVAILABLE FROM BLOOMSBURY

A Critical Introduction to Testimony, Axel Gelfert

Epistemology: The Key Thinkers, Stephen Hetherington

Metaphysics, Alexander Baumgarten (translated and
edited by Courtney D. Fugate and John Hymers)

Relativism: A Guide for the Perplexed, Timothy M. Mosteller

Relativism in Contemporary American Philosophy,
Timothy M. Mosteller

Truth and Method, Hans-Georg Gadamer

Theories of Truth: An Introduction

TIMOTHY M. MOSTELLER

B L O O M S B U R Y

LONDON · NEW DELHI · NEW YORK · SYDNEY

Bloomsbury Academic
An imprint of Bloomsbury Publishing Plc

50 Bedford Square	1385 Broadway
London	New York
WC1B 3DP	NY 10018
UK	USA

www.bloomsbury.com

Bloomsbury is a registered trade mark of Bloomsbury Publishing Plc

First published 2014

© Timothy M. Mosteller, 2014

Timothy M. Mosteller has asserted his right under the Copyright,
Designs and Patents Act, 1988, to be identified as the Author of this work.

British Library Cataloguing-in-Publication Data
A catalogue record for this book is available from the British Library.

ISBN: HB: 978-1-4411-6356-1
PB: 978-1-4411-1969-8
ePDF: 978-1-4411-7084-2
ePub: 978-1-4411-9196-0

Library of Congress Cataloging-in-Publication Data
A catalog record for this book is available from the Library of Congress.

Typeset by Integra Software Services Pvt. Ltd.
Printed and bound in India

To Jacob Edward and Katherine Sophia in true love
In memory of Dallas Willard (1935–2013), a true mentor

Contents

> Sept. 29th
> My seminar.

Contents

Acknowledgments

This book could not have been written without a generous research grant from Earhart Foundation for the 2012–2013 academic year. I am very grateful for the foundation's support for this project.

I am especially grateful for the generous support of the International Academy of Philosophy – Edith Stein Institute in Granada, Spain, for providing a quiet and contemplative office from which much of my writing, reading, and thinking was done. I am also especially grateful to Josef Seifert, Marcelo Cambronero, Mátyás Szalay, and Guillermo Bautista for welcoming me to the institute and for their encouraging comments on this work.

I am indebted to María José Frápolli and the Department of Philosophy at the University of Granada, Spain, for the use of their academic library. I am grateful for being welcomed into their scholarly community and for the ability to participate in their department's research seminars and colloquia during my sabbatical stay. I am particularly thankful for helpful comments provided for portions of the chapter on pragmatism which I was able to present to their faculty.

I want to thank Eddie Colanter, Robbie Hirsch, and Josh Rasmussen for reading and commenting on several draft chapters of the manuscript. I am grateful for their philosophical camaraderie.

I wish to extend thanks to the President and Board of Trustees at California Baptist University for the sabbatical leave grant during which most of this book was written. I am especially grateful for the support of my Dean, Chris Morgan, and my colleagues Scott Key and Todd Bates.

This work would not have been possible without the influence of Dallas Willard to whose memory this book is dedicated. His views on the nature of truth and the ontology of knowledge have shaped my approach to truth presented in this book. I hope that I have been his faithful student.

Introduction

In preparing to write this book, I often read from philosophers of different schools that everyday truths like, "My keys are on my desk" are obvious, trivial, and therefore uninformative to developing a robust account of truth. This didn't seem quite right to me. Why not begin with the data of our commonsense experiences of truth and develop our account of truth from there? This book is an attempt to introduce you to theories of truth by doing just that.

Think of this book as a guided tour through a museum. I begin the tour by reflecting on our commonsense understanding of truth and proceed to examine various theories of truth in light of this knowledge. As with any museum tour, there is usually a lot more in the museum than either the tourist or the guide is able to take in at one particular time. As your tour guide, I am only introducing you to parts of "the collection" of theories of truth. There are galleries upon galleries in this philosophical museum about truth that I do not even mention, let alone comment upon. On this particular tour, I highlight only some of the ideas and some of the problems of what I take to be the salient approaches to truth that have been influential in recent years. It is my hope that from this introduction you will be able to think carefully, clearly, and truly about any other approach to truth or particular problems in an approach to truth on your next visit to the museum.

As your tour guide, I must admit that I am opinionated. Just as a guide through an art museum might believe that impressionism is a more beautiful style than cubism, or that Michelangelo was a superior painter than Pollock, I too believe that some theories of truth are better than others. I believe that some claims about truth are themselves true and that others are false. I also believe that some of my own claims about truth could be false! (I do hope that I've not asserted any false claims in this book, but it is possible!)

In the first chapter, I give a brief defense of this commonsense notion of truth and argue that truth is neither physical nor linguistic. I proceed to show how truth fits into an overall study of philosophy, and give a brief history of truth from antiquity to today. The bulk of the book is dedicated to examining the major theories of truth which have been defended in the last 120 years or so. The latter part of this book involves my own philosophical reflections about truth and metaphysics and how truth applies to other areas outside of philosophy. I present some reasons to think that a realistic, commonsense view of a correspondence account of truth is the true way to understand truth, and that this approach to truth has strong implications for other areas of human inquiry.

Leading this tour is of particular personal importance for me as a teacher of philosophy to undergraduate students. One of my first tasks when teaching any philosophy class is to show my students that relativism about truth is highly problematic. Having written against relativism elsewhere, I seek now to pursue an account of truth that is non-relativistic, objective, and clear, which can be found by anyone who loves wisdom. Regardless of whether you are persuaded in what follows, I hope that you will agree that we can know the truth, and the truth will set us free.

1

Truth and Philosophy

1.1 Truth is simple

I reach for my keys in my backpack to unlock my car. They are not there. I believe that I have left my keys on my desk. I return to my office. (The secretary lets me in for the third time this semester.) I look on my desk. I see my keys. I swipe them off the desk, mumble my apologies again to the secretary, call my wife to let her know I'll be late (again), and head to my car.

Since I'm in a rush to get home, I'm not in a particularly philosophically reflective mood, but something commonly extraordinary just occurred. This profound yet mundane event occurs countless times for every human being capable of having everyday experiences. I knew truth. I experienced truth. Truth was immediately present in my experience.

Recognizing this experience of truth is neither to maintain that truth is nothing more than an individual experience, nor to deny that truth is independent from an individual experience. It is simply to say that truth can be understood from our common experiences. Truth is simple. Truth is fully present in our experiences. We can know truth. This is an easy place for us to begin our inquiry about truth.

Suppose that I weren't in a rush to get home. Suppose I were to reflect philosophically on what just happened. Suppose I engage in what C. S. Peirce called *ideoscopy*.[1] Suppose we pay close attention to what actually goes on in our own experiences. By looking at our experience of truth (the match between our minds and reality), we can glean insight into truth. Paying attention to our experiences allows us to give an *assay* of truth, an examination of the characteristics of our simple experience of finding the world as it was thought to be. In this case, we want to know the characteristics of the experience of seeing the keys on the desk match directly our belief that the keys are on the desk.

When it comes to analyzing the everyday experience of experiencing truth, there are at least four primary parts to that experience: (1) there is our own self who has beliefs and experiences, (2) we have beliefs about where the car keys are, (3) we have a sensory experience of seeing our keys on our desk, and (4) we have an empirical experience of seeing that "my sensory experience of the keys on the desk" matches the belief that the keys are on the desk. These four things serve as the primary objects of study for our analysis of our experience of truth.

1.1.1 *Truth is not physical*

In our examination of our simple experiences of truth, we begin with ourselves. That is not to say that truth is dependent on us, but it is to say that in our common experiences of truth, we are first aware of ourselves as the kinds of beings who can experience truth. We are the kinds of beings who can come to experience the world matching our beliefs. What kind of thing must we be if we are to make sense of our ordinary experiences of truth? According to St. Thomas Aquinas and Aristotle long before him, truth is possible in our experiences because the soul exists and in some way can "become" all things. This means that we can conceive of ourselves as souls with intellectual capacities for beliefs about the world and experiences of the world. When experience and belief match, we experience truth. While a complete account of the human soul is a bit beyond the scope of this book, in order for us to elaborate on our common experiences of finding the world as it is believed to be, a few things must be true about the soul.

First, it must exist and be the kind of thing which has capacities to believe, remember, act, experience, and understand. I take it to be obvious, that without an entity such as the soul, the account of truth we are sketching would be impossible. Without a subject capable of having an intellect that could be conformed to reality, there can be no conformity at all. In other words, if truth is essentially a relation between the intellect and reality, then if there were no intellects, then there could be no experience of truth.

Second, and this is much debated in contemporary philosophy, the soul cannot be a thing which is material. Here are two brief arguments as to why. We have experiences of finding our beliefs matching reality. We are aware of our beliefs being about the way things are. This "being about" things is often called "intentionality." Intentionality is a property of beliefs. It is the property of being about something. So, given our awareness of our own beliefs and given that our beliefs possess the property of intentionality, it is possible to see whether any material thing could possess such a property. If not, then what we are aware of, when we are aware of our beliefs, is not something that is material.

Here is the argument:

P1. No physical states are essentially intentional states.

P2. All things having mental states (including beliefs) are essentially intentional states (i.e., are about something).

C1. No things having mental states are physical states.

P2 is nearly a definition. The controversial premise here is P1, physical states are excluded from the category of essentially intentional states. The justification for P1 is this. If a physical state were intentional, it would need some additional thing to "read" or understand what its intentional state is about. For any physical state, the possibility for it to be understood as an intentional state would require an interpreter, such an interpreter could not be another physical state, which would require an interpreter for it. Thus, in order to avoid an infinite regress, an un-interpreted interpreter of the intentional state (if such a thing were possible) would be required. Such a thing philosophers have called the soul.

To extend the argument further, we need the following:

P3. All human souls are things having mental states.

P4. No physical states are things having mental states (from C1 via conversion).

C2. No human souls are physical states.

If the evidence for P4 above is reasonable, then this argument might need some justification for P3. P3 is at least self-evident for a human soul which is thinking. Descartes was quite right about this. Maintaining P3 is not to deny the possibility of a human soul existing without actualizing mental states. So, perhaps a distinction could be made in the middle term here of this argument, "things having mental states." We could distinguish, following Aristotle,[2] two ways of having mental states: in potentiality or in actuality. P3 refers to actuality, but this is not to deny having mental states in potentiality, which, again following Aristotle, are ontologically necessary for having mental states in actuality. So, in conclusion, the soul is the kind of thing which can have mental states in actuality and is non-material.

A different approach to thinking that the soul is immaterial can be considered from an argument from logical normativity. This is a reduction argument to the absurdity of reducing logical mental states to brain states. What this argument is supposed to show is that if the soul (or at least its rational faculty) were material, then logic itself would be based on something irrational. Even worse, if one argued that the rational faculty of the soul were material, the basis of that argument would ultimately be irrational.

Consider two examples of basic logical reasoning with each statement identified with a particular brain state.

I. *Modus Ponens*		*Modus Ponens* **physicalized**
1. If p then q	$\rightarrow$	Brain State 1 (BS1)
2. p	$\rightarrow$	BS2
3. Therefore, q	$\rightarrow$	BS3

II. *Denying Antecedent*   *Denying Antecedent* **physicalized**

1. * If p then q →   BS1*

2. * not-p →   BS2*

3. * not-q →   BS3*

My claim is that if the soul were material, then *modus ponens* and *denying antecedent* are each nothing more than exemplifications of brain states. If they are nothing more than brain states, then there is no non-arbitrary reason for maintaining that 3 logically follows from 1 and 2, while 3* does not follow from 1* and 3*. If all mental states are reducible to brain states, then why should it be more reasonable to desire to have BS3 rather than BS3*? How does one non-arbitrarily maintain that one brain state is more reasonable to have than another? The thing is impossible. If the rational part of the soul were material, then there is no non-arbitrary way to do logic, other than a mere language game. But, surely we can see, by means of rational insight that 3 follows from 1 and 2, while 3* does not follow from 1* and 2*. Therefore, the soul cannot be entirely material. Therefore, our first main feature of our assay of our experience of truth is ourselves as immaterial beings, as intellects capable of having our minds conformed to reality.

Let us consider again our original example. When I went out to my car, the immaterial part of me came to a realization that I had forgot my keys (again). My intellect then formed (with a little bit of memory searching) a belief that my keys were on my desk. But, what exactly is a belief? There are a few obvious things about beliefs. (1) Beliefs are mental states based upon thoughts. (2) Beliefs are about something. They have intentionality. (3) Beliefs are springboards to action. If I believe something, I am doing more than just thinking about something. For example, there is a difference between thinking about there being a live, angry, venomous rattlesnake in my backpack, and believing that there is a live, angry, venomous rattlesnake in my backpack. The difference between thinking and believing is that believing involves my willingness to act as if what I am thinking about really were the case; that is, really were true. This is not to say that beliefs are nothing more than our actions. That would be similar to the psychological view of behaviorism which identifies belief as a form of action. I do not accept this view, because someone of course can have a belief and never express their belief in action, but a belief is like a springboard to action. We ought to say as well that we should be aware that belief and truth are quite different from one another. I might believe that there is a rattlesnake in my backpack and demonstrate this by my actions toward my backpack, but the truth of my belief is going to depend on whether there really is a rattlesnake in my backpack. This leads us to the final feature of beliefs. (4) Beliefs can be the bearers of truth. They can *be* true or false depending on whether they match the way the world is.

I reach for my keys because I believe that they are in my backpack; I realize that they are not there; I form the belief that they are on my desk. This belief is: (1) a thought in my immaterial mind, (2) about the world (my keys being on my desk), (3) which gives me a disposition to act (to walk back to my office and look at my desk), and (4) will either match or not match the reality which it is about.

Now that this belief has been formed in my mind, I can use it to direct myself back to my office in order to look to see if reality matches my belief. As I open the door to my office, and survey my (surprisingly tidy for this point in the semester) desk, I see my keys on my desk. This is an act of perception which involves my mind coming to experience a bit of reality. While there is a whole corpus of literature on perception, we have all had perceptions of things which served as the basis of our knowing those things.[3] There is something unique about this perception. It is not a passive perception. It is not something that simply occurs because of my perceptive faculties. This perception is one that I am anticipating, expecting, or looking for. Given my belief that my keys are on my desk, it is natural to expect to find them where I believed them to be. Much of what we perceive is not something we are actively expecting. I might perceive how chilly it is in this office. I might perceive the distant noise of traffic on the street, but I am not currently intending to experience those things. They are not on the active horizon of my expectations given the beliefs that I have. However, in this experience, I have a perception that I am actively intending to perceive. This active intention to perceive that my keys are on my desk contributes to my experience of finding (or not finding) my keys to be where they were believed to be. Expecting to find my keys where I believed them to be heightens the experience of truth when it is experienced.

The final part of our survey happens when we experience truth. This is the experience of the matching between reality and belief. In some ways this is the result of my activity of looking for my keys because of my belief, but it is really quite a passive thing. I do not make the belief true. There is nothing I can do to get the belief and reality to match up. Once I form the belief, I either experience reality matching the belief, or I experience reality not matching the belief. Now, of course I can change reality to match my belief. For example, I could grab the keys off the floor and throw them on the desk... "Aha! I made my belief that the keys were on the desk true!" But this is trivial. I could change my beliefs to match reality after I experience reality... "I now believe that my keys are locked in the car" after I see that they are not on my desk. This is well and good, but in neither case do I actively make the belief that my keys are on the desk true. I am a passive recipient of that truth when I experience the matching (or lack of matching) of my beliefs with reality.

When I had a belief that my keys were on my desk, and I used that belief to guide me to the place where I believed my keys to be, and I saw that my keys were where I believed them to be, then, just at that moment, I knew truth. I had a belief in my mind about the way the world is. I had a direct empirical, visual experience of my keys being on my desk. I experienced the matching of my beliefs with my keys. This analysis of truth is quite simple. Perhaps, I have never heard the word "truth" before or even gave any philosophical thought to the idea of truth. Yet, the moment I experience the matching of my belief about my keys being on my desk with the reality of my keys being on my desk, I experience truth. I know truth.[4] I may give no thought to this experience. I may never reflect upon what has just happened. Yet, in that moment, I have available for my mind to reflect upon an experience of truth. We have experience and knowledge of truth countless times in our lives. We have before our minds the possibility to reflect upon and consider philosophically the matching of our beliefs with reality. In this way, truth is one of the simplest things that could ever occur to anyone. Truth is obvious in our ordinary experiences. Dallas Willard had pointed out that truth is so obvious, that we never have to teach kids how to lie (Willard 1999b).

1.1.2 *Truth is not linguistic*

I think about where I left my keys. I form a belief about my keys being on my desk. I use this thought to guide myself to where I believe my keys are. I see my keys on the desk exactly as I believed them to be. I see my belief of the keys being on the desk conforming to reality of the keys being on the desk. I see the truth of my belief.

I take this to be a paradigm case of truth. If one wants to understand the concept of truth, one simply needs to exercise careful reflective analysis of these common everyday experiences. Some recent theorists of truth maintain that understanding the concept of truth requires only an analysis of our use of language and "truth talk." The emphasis in these theories is that somehow truth is linguistic in nature. Here is an example:

> It will become clearer as the argument of the book progresses that a full understanding of the meaning of higher order concepts— truth is only one among them—requires a reflective and highly developed understanding of the different things that rational agents **do with words**.
>
> (Frápolli 2012, p. 2, emphasis added)

I believe that it is a mistake to identify or reduce a theory of truth to a theory of language, or to identify truth with language. Here is why. In the simple example above regarding finding my car keys, I have thought many things. I have believed many things. I have even acted because of my beliefs. What I have not done is said, written, spoken, uttered, texted, tweeted, or used language in any way. I certainly could have said, "My keys are on my desk." I could have texted my wife, "i left keys on desk LOL B home late LUV U :)." In the case at hand, I did none of these things. I simply thought, believed, looked, and saw. None of the mental acts in this case involve the use of language in any way. If this is correct, then not only is truth independent from language, but our experience and knowledge of truth does not depend upon language. Thus, a theory of truth can neither be reduced to linguistics nor does a theory of truth even require an appeal to language.

Here is the simple argument for the position I am maintaining.

P1. All intellectual acts are thoughts.

P2. No thoughts are linguistic acts.

C1. Therefore, no linguistic acts are intellectual acts.

P4. All experiences of truth are intellectual acts.

P5. No intellectual acts are linguistic acts.

C2. Therefore, no experiences of truth are linguistic acts.

The major objection to this argument will likely focus on P2. The objection will likely maintain that some of our mental states are linguistic entities. However, according to Dallas Willard, "the very conception of thinking in or with language involves an absurdity" (Willard 1973, p. 126). Let us examine the argument for this view.

Willard comes to this conclusion by distinguishing thinking from language. First, thoughts are intentional states of persons (they are *of* or *about* something). Second, language always involves "sense perceptible signs or symbols" (p. 128) and "*some* level of actual sensuous apprehension of the signs" when language is used. Willard claims that it is very easy to produce cases where thought occurs without the presence of language. The case considered here of thinking of where my keys are or thinking about my belief matching reality is just such a case. There are no physical signs here at all in these cases of thinking. If there are no physical signs, then no language is present. Thus, Willard concludes that we have here a "proof that thinking is *not* essentially the activity of operating with signs" (p. 129).

Willard continues to argue that if we think with language, then we must be doing something "*with* symbols, and so necessarily involves doing something *to* them" (p. 131). Yet, there are clear cases of thought where we don't do anything to or with signs, "there not being any signs in these cases" (p. 131). Willard summarizes this point by saying that thought alone, "mere thinking" cannot do anything "*to* signs" and thus can't do anything "*with* signs" (p. 131). Therefore, thought is not linguistic. If Willard's argument is sufficient to show that no thoughts are linguistic acts, then, the second premise of this argument is reasonable.

One might argue against premise P1 by claiming that there are some intellectual acts which are not thoughts. However, the emphasis on this premise should be *act*. An act of the intellect is something that I do with my mind. I do not mean here a state of the mind, but an activity of the mind. An activity of the mind will always have thought as an essential component. Thus, intellectual acts are acts of thought.

Willard's argument could, I believe, be broadened to show that no mental states at all are linguistic. For if Willard is right that all linguistic entities have essentially as their nature physical signs or symbols, and it can be argued that no mental states are physical states, then it would follow that no mental states are linguistic entities. This would be a stronger support for the idea put forward here that truth (understood as conformity of thing and intellect) does not involve language.

Suffice it to say that we have clear cases of experiencing the world as we thought it to be. These experiences involving thought do not make use of language, nor is thought itself ever linguistic. Thus, a theory of truth, or the meaning of truth will not require as an essential component a theory or philosophy of language.

1.2 Where is truth?

While I have just outlined and partly argued that truth is simply present in our common everyday experiences of finding the world the way we believed it to be, we might want to know where truth is located. By "located," I don't mean spatially or physically. I mean, where is it located within the discipline of philosophy?

If you are reading this book as a philosophy student, you are probably familiar with the meaning of the word "philosophy" which is Greek in origin and literally means "love of wisdom." It is interesting that philosophy as it has been practiced since ancient times is called the love of wisdom and not the love of truth. I suppose that would be called "philalethia" (*phila*: love, *alethia*: truth). This raises the question of how truth and the love of wisdom are related.

The idea of loving wisdom needs to be disambiguated. When we say "love" in English we use the word very loosely. You can see this confusion in "I ♥" bumper stickers and T-shirts. Maybe you've seen "I ♥ My Poodle" or "I ♥ Grandma" (usually on Grandma's car) or "I ♥ Jesus." Suppose you saw all three of these stickers on the *same* car in the parking lot at work! What would you think? Yep, the person sure has a lot of love in their heart. But what else would you think? Hopefully the person behind the wheel doesn't "love" these three things in the exact same ways. One of these objects of "love" they worship, the other they visit for cookies, and the still other they scoop up after when they take them for walks. Hopefully, the right sort of love goes with the right object of love. Thankfully, the Greek language has several different words for love: *storge, agape, eros,* and *philo.*[5]

Storge is affection. Affection is a kind of love which is sentimental and can be applied toward lots of different kinds of things, from comfortable shoes, to colleagues to ice cream. These are things we generally *like* and with which we are affectionate. This kind of love expresses the things we enjoy and are comfortable with. *Storge* (affection) is distinct from *philo* (friendship) in that it does not require any commonality. I can have affection for a coworker, even though we don't have much of anything in common. We get along, we like one another, but we are not friends. This doesn't diminish the relationship; it is just in its own unique category.

Agape is unconditional love. It is often thought of as divine love. The kind of love that is patient, kind, does not demand its own way, bears all things, and believes all things is forgiving—no matter what.[6] This is the most powerful type of love possible. *Agape* is distinct from *philo*. When *agape* love is put into practice, it does not require reciprocity. The person toward whom I am showing unconditional *agape* love need not respond in kind to me for the *agape* love I am expressing to be real. Indeed, those who are able to love people unconditionally, no matter what wrongs they are suffered, are not necessarily friends with those whom they love, but the *agape* love they are expressing is real indeed. Practicing this kind of love in the workplace can radically transform a hostile working environment, or one of unhealthy cutthroat competition, into a place of mutual cooperation and trust. It's hard to do.

Eros is "lover's love" or the kind of love that lovers are in. If you've ever been in love, you know exactly what it is like. It is a pure desire for unity with the beloved. If you are "in love" in the sense of *eros*, you find yourself simply lost in your beloved. Lovers spend time gazing *at* one another, desiring one another, staring into one another's eyes, time standing still. *Eros* is distinct from *philo* in this way: lovers are always seen face to face, but friends are always seen side to side. Lovers simply desire one another. Friends desire something other than their own relationship. Most friends, unlike lovers, don't spend time talking about their friendship. Most friends don't say things like, "We need to talk about us." Lovers do! If you find yourself staring into the eyes of your friend for a prolonged time, you may need to have a little talk with your friend, because something more is most certainly going on in the relationship!

Philo or friendship is distinct from these other types of love in three ways. First, friendship, unlike *storge* involves commonality. Friendship is always about something. Friends are friends because they have something in common. It is hard to imagine having a friend with whom you have literally nothing in common. Friendship involves common activities which can range from being fans of a football team to pursuing a political cause, to common career goals or interests. Without common interests or activities, friendships soon fade. Second, friendship unlike *agape* requires reciprocity. Friendships are *two way* relationships. You can't be friend with someone unless the friendship is mutual. It's probably why adults don't go around asking people at work if they will be their friend. Third, friendship is always about something, usually things you *do* with your friend, common activities.

What then is *sophia*? She is wisdom. If friendship is a relationship with common activities directed toward a goal, how do I have a *friendship* with *wisdom*? "Wisdom" sounds like a concept or an idea, which doesn't seem like the kind of thing that I can be friends with. It doesn't seem like I can be friends with something other than a person. Often, you hear people say things which sound like we can be friends with material objects. People say things like, "If there's a fire in your house, a fire extinguisher is your best friend" or "In the heat of battle, a good rifle is a soldier's best friend." You also hear people say things which sound like we can be friends with animals, "A dog is a man's best friend." I think that these senses of friendship are derivative from real friendship which we know primarily as something that we have with other people. Friendship is something personal; it's something that goes on only between persons. If this is right, then *philosophy* or friendship with wisdom is going to be a friendship between you and *wisdom*, where wisdom is understood as a person, or something personal.

For us in the twenty-first century, it's hard to imagine being friends with wisdom. However, in the ancient world, wisdom was thought to be a person or like a person, someone with whom you could have a friendship. For example, the ancient Jewish philosopher King Solomon conceived of wisdom as a woman who was present in your life to give you guidance and direction. She would call out to those in need of direction and encourage them to follow her counsel. Solomon's Book of Proverbs puts it like this:

Does not wisdom call out? Does not understanding raise her voice? On the heights along the way, where the paths meet, she takes her stand; beside the gates leading into the city, at the entrances, she cries aloud: "To you, O men, I call out; I raise my voice to all mankind. You who are simple, gain prudence; you who are foolish, gain understanding. Listen, for I have worthy things to say…Choose my instruction instead of silver, knowledge rather than choice gold, for wisdom is more precious than rubies, and nothing you desire can compare with her."

(Proverbs 8:1–4, Holy Bible 1993)

The ancient Romans also understood philosophy as a person. In the sixth century A.D., a philosopher named Anicius Manlius Severinus Boëthius wrote about Lady Philosophy who appeared to him while he was imprisoned and awaiting execution for a crime he didn't commit. He describes her as, "She was of awe-inspiring appearance, her eyes burning and keen beyond the usual power of men. She was so full of years that I could hardly think of her as of my own generation, and yet she possessed a vivid colour and undiminished vigour" (Boethius 1999, pp. 3–4). If we are to understand the views of truth from the ancient writers which we are going to meet in the next chapter, we too are going to have to open our minds to the possibility that *Sophia-Wisdom* is a person with whom we can have a friendship.

If we are open to seeing Wisdom as a person, and we enter into a friendship with her, then there will be common activities that we *do* with her. Those common activities will be directed toward the goal of human well-being and doing. There are three activities that we do have in common with Sophia. These activities are three "ologies" or "studies of" something: ontology, epistemology, and axiology. These are the three common activities that philosophers down through the ages have recognized as key ingredients to living well and doing well, whether in our work or in life.

The first, ontology, the study of (ology) *being or existence* (*on*), is the study of the ultimate nature of reality. If you are an ontologist, you will ask questions like: What is real? What really exists? Some philosophers answer these questions by saying that ultimate reality is something physical or reducible to the categories of the physical sciences. These people are also known as materialists or physicalists. Other philosophers believe that reality is entirely spiritual or mental. These thinkers are known as idealists. Ontology is crucial to the whole purpose of philosophy. The question of the nature of reality and the existential status of human beings has profound effects on how we live.

How does truth connect with ontology or metaphysics? There are two ways to think about this. First, there is a metaphysics of truth. Truth itself is something real. It has being. Take for instance the example we began with at the beginning of this chapter: the experience of finding the world as we believed it to be. This act is a *real* thing. Given its reality, it can be studied. It has its own metaphysics which can be analyzed in a careful and systematic way.

Second, there is truth about metaphysics. Any overarching metaphysics, that is, a complete account of the nature of reality will itself be the kind of thing which matches (or fails to match) the way the world really is. The example we started with which we began the chapter, the belief that "my keys are on my desk," is fundamentally no different than a belief that "all of reality is spiritual." It is no different in the sense that both beliefs are about the world, and both beliefs will either match or not match the reality that they are about. They will either be true or false. Of course, finding the truth of where my keys are located is going to be much easier than finding a grand theory of the ultimate nature of reality. Yet, finding the truth about metaphysics is fundamentally the same: it is a matter of looking at the reality in question and seeing if it matches the belief. So, any metaphysical theory or total ontology will be true or false. Thus, there is truth about metaphysics (ontology) as well as a metaphysics (ontology) of truth.

The second activity which we have in common in our friendship with wisdom is epistemology. Epistemology is the study of knowledge. Epistemologists ask questions like these: What is knowledge? What can we know? What's the difference between having an opinion about something and really knowing it? What is the extent or scope of human knowledge? People make a big deal today about living in a "knowledge economy." Hardly anyone is able to say what knowledge is. It isn't found by "Googling" up an answer to a question, and it's not located in Wikipedia, as good and useful as both of these are.

It is in the philosophical activity of epistemology that is the proper home of an analysis of truth. Truth does have its own metaphysics and, as we will see below, its own value. In fact, all of these are areas of philosophy: ontology, epistemology, and axiology (ethics and esthetics) are intimately united, and I believe inseparable. Why is truth generally a part of epistemology? One reason is that truth is connected with what we believe. As I mentioned above, beliefs are the kinds of things that are true or false. Beliefs of course play a large role in our claims to know things. In fact, as you may know, one of the classic definitions of knowledge that has come down to us from ancient times is that knowledge is a belief that is justified and true (or justified true belief). In an analysis or theory of knowledge, one wants to know not only what justification or evidence someone has for their beliefs but whether those beliefs are true. Do the beliefs match reality? So, an account of truth is part and parcel of an account of knowledge.

There is also an epistemology of truth. It is a perfectly reasonable and intelligible question to ask, "How do you know what truth is?" This is an epistemological question that pertains to truth as an object of inquiry. To give an example of this (we will be pursuing this question throughout this book), consider the case we began the chapter with. One might answer the question, "How do you know what truth is?" by simply appealing to one's own experience of truth, of finding the world to be as one believed it to be. Truth is the kind of thing that not only has being (i.e., pertains to ontology) but also can be known (i.e., pertains to epistemology).

A third activity of philosophy is axiology, or the study of value. An axiologist will seek answers to questions like, what kinds of things are valuable? Are things valuable because we value them, or do we value things because they are valuable? The discipline of axiology can be divided into the study of non-moral values, which is the discipline of esthetics, and the study of moral values, which is the discipline of ethics. Both of these disciplines are related to truth.

The discipline of esthetics is the study of beauty. Estheticians ask questions like, What is beauty? What makes a work of art or a work of nature beautiful? Is beauty in the eye of the beholder? Like ontology and epistemology, there will be truth in any esthetic theory. One's account of the nature of beauty will either match or not match up with reality. It will either be true or false.

Is there an esthetics of truth? There may be. Take our first example of finding my keys on my desk. Suppose this is an instance of truth. It has being and can be known, but is it beautiful? If beauty involves order and specified realization of the way things are, then yes, truth has a certain beauty to it.

In addition to esthetics, ethics is a central part of axiology. Ethics is the pinnacle of philosophy. It seeks answers to the questions, what is the good life, and who is the good person? What kind of life is worth living? Does the good life mean giving all of your money away, taking a vow of poverty and joining the Peace Corps? Does the good life mean acquiring as much wealth as possible before you die? Who is a good person? Who should I want to be like? These are the questions of ethics. Ethicists seek to answer these types of questions. Your view of ethics determines how you live and what kind of person you are.

There is clearly a truth to ethics. Ethical views either match reality or fail to match. Someone once said that truth is what you run into when you are wrong. This is especially obvious in ethical theories of how to live our lives.

There is also an ethics to truth. Truth is good, morally good. Truth helps us live our lives well. In this sense, truth is valuable. To make this clear, you might consider two lives. One life maintains a commitment to truth. The other life does not. Is it even possible to call a life good or worth living if there is a total absence for a concern for truth? On a purely practical level, it seems obvious that the answer is, No! How would you even make it through the day if you had no concern as to whether it was true that the clock was correct or true that the bus leaves at 8 a.m. or true that you are supposed to show up to work by 9:00? Truth helps us deal effectively with reality.[7] Truth helps us come to know what is good in the way to live and to be as human beings.

Philosophy and the activities of ontology, epistemology, and axiology affect everything we do. As I have argued, one's account of truth is intimately intertwined with one's view of reality, knowledge, goodness, and beauty. Our basic philosophical views will affect our views in all areas of life. Philosophers recognize that there are various "philosophies of," in which your view of ontology, epistemology, and axiology together with your view of truth deeply impacts your commitments in other major areas of life. For example, the philosophy of science is one such "philosophy of." What is science? This question cannot be answered in a lab, or by various scientific experiments. It is a philosophical question. Philosophy of religion is another example, in which questions like "Does God exist?" are raised and answered using the tools of the discipline of philosophy. Philosophies of literature, philosophy of politics, philosophy of history, philosophy of mathematics, philosophy of mind, and philosophy of business are other examples as well.

Let me make this clearer with a few examples. If you think that reality is physical, this is going to affect your view about religions. Religious experience and religious knowledge obtained from it will be explained through various sense perceptions traceable to empirical sensory inputs rather than to the activity of a deity in human affairs. Similarly, if you have a "philosophy of medicine" in which you maintain from one's ethics that human beings are not intrinsically valuable, then you might conclude that various medical practices, in which human beings who are of no use to society, for example, persons in vegetative states, can be experimented on for the greater good of others who are suffering. It is important to note that any "philosophy of" will be deeply informed by underlying ontological, epistemological, and ethical views.

In summary, a philosopher will enter into various activities with wisdom. These activities include ontology, epistemology (particularly a study of truth for our purposes in this book), and axiology. Each of these activities is pursued with an eye as to how one can practice in one's life the art of well-being and well-doing. Of course, it is possible to learn *about* truth, ontology, epistemology, and axiology. This may have gotten you through an intro to philosophy class, if you had one in college. Knowing about philosophy and truth is necessary but not a sufficient condition for well-being and well-doing. Remember, philosophy, in the very meaning of the word is a friendship with wisdom, not a mere study of wisdom. Studying truth, which is what we will do in this book, is not the essence of philosophy. You can have a great theory of truth...maybe even the best theory ever put forward, but this does not make you a friend of wisdom. That sort of relationship means appropriating not only the truth of the theories that you have discovered in the areas of ontology, epistemology, and axiology, but it means living out what is true, loving what is true as one loves one's friends. Friendship with wisdom begins with a love of truth.

1.3 Overview of the book

This book then can be seen as a guide to love truth in order to be friends with wisdom, to be a philosopher. Here is a brief sketch of what is to follow in the remaining chapters of this book.

In Chapter 2, "A Short History of Truth," we will examine the idea of truth in the history of philosophy from the pre-Socratics to the twenty-first century. It treats each of the major periods in the history of philosophy including: the Greco-Roman, Medieval, and Modern and Contemporary period of philosophy. I will argue that the dominant theory of truth in the history of philosophy has been some version of a correspondence theory.

In Chapters 3–7, we will analyze four major approaches to truth: coherence, pragmatic, deflationist, and correspondence theories. Each of these approaches will be articulated, compared, and assessed.

In Chapter 8, I return to what I take to be a paradigm case of truth with which we began this chapter. In this chapter, I put forward my own account of how truth should be understood. In particular, I will focus on how truth is understood from a commonsense perspective that requires a commitment to a particular view of the nature of reality, namely realism about universals. I will develop my account using the resources of correspondence theories of truth and show how commonsense realism about truth provides us with an account of truth that makes the most sense out of our ordinary experiences of truth.

I conclude the book in Chapter 9 by showing how a commonsense view of truth applies to, freedom, economics, and religion. First, I argue that understanding a commonsense view of truth can be the foundation of our awareness of individual and political liberty. Second, I argue that truth is crucial to a flourishing economic life. That a theory of truth applies to economic life not only at the individual level in virtues such as honesty and integrity, but also at a systemic level in areas such as trust and cooperation. Third, I argue that religious claims can be true or false, and that we can come to see the truth of religious claims in the same way that we come to see the truth of our beliefs in ordinary experiences.

2

A Short History of Truth

2.1 A short history of truth

As I argued in Chapter 1, philosophical reflection about truth is connected with every area of philosophy. The way we think about truth affects and is affected by our ontology, epistemology, ethics, esthetics, and logic. Philosophy of truth also extends from these areas of philosophy to other areas outside of philosophy. In the final chapters of this book, we will investigate how a theory of truth connects with thinking about science, religion, politics, and business.

When studying philosophy, students often take whole courses in the history of philosophy. In a typical undergraduate program in philosophy this is usually composed of several survey courses that are typically divided between ancient, medieval, modern, postmodern, and contemporary philosophy. In this chapter, I present a brief survey of a few examples of philosophical reflection on truth from these major periods. The historical division is meant to follow a typical division of the history of philosophy as it is often taught in philosophy majors in

American universities. This historical division is a bit arbitrary. Ideas continue over long periods of time. They often overlap our divisions of history. There are often no clear-cut lines by means of which to sharply divide one historical period from another. While this may be, I intend to show that philosophical reflection on truth has been fairly uniform throughout most of the history of philosophy up until the nineteenth, twentieth, and early twenty-first centuries.

2.2 Ancient Literature

In ancient Greek and Hebrew literature there are frequent uses of the idea of truth, *alethia* in Greek and *emeth* in Hebrew. In this section, I will point out a few things about these ideas which will be useful for my case that truth is important for human life (as I argued in the previous chapter and will argue in the chapter at the end of the book on an application of truth to various aspects of human life). In addition, these ideas also give us some reason to believe that ancient writers understood and recognized the commonsense notion of truth as correspondence with reality.

In ancient Greek literature, for example, Hesiods' *Works and Days* and Homer's *Iliad* and *Odyssey*, there are several references to truth. An example of the use of *alethia* in Hesiod is in the *Works and Days*, when he writes, "Mark the days which come from Zeus, duly telling your slaves of them." (Hesiod 11:765). "Duly" in this translation is directly from the Greek "alethia" or truth. Hesiod here is indicating that the righteous man will speak what is true, and tell how things really are regarding the days which the gods have given to men.

There are several uses of the idea of truth (*alethia* in Greek) in the *Iliad*. In the great chariot race in the *Iliad*, Homer uses the word "truth" when he refers to Phoenix who is to be an umpire in the race so that he can "mark the running and tell the truth thereof" (Homer 1924, line 23:360). When someone judges reality, they are looking for the truth, for the way things really are.

In another place in the *Iliad*, Homer presents Priam searching for the body of his dead son Hector among the Greeks, and he asks Achilles' squire to tell him "all the truth [*alethia*]" about Hector's body, whether it has been preserved or cut to pieces and given to the dogs. In other words, Priam is looking for what is real, and expects to be told about how things really are. He is asked to be told the truth (Homer 1924, 24:4).

Another Homeric example of the use of alethia is found in the *Odyssey*. Odysseus is granted an audience with the dead and is able to converse with the shade of Achilles. As he converses with the shade of Achilles, Odysseus tells Achilles that he will speak the truth (*alethia*) about Achilles' son Neoptolemus (Homer 1919, 11:486). Odysseus is going to tell Achilles about what is real. His words are going to reflect what really occurred in the history of Neoptolemus' life.

In each of these cases, we see examples of truth understood as a correspondence of belief to reality. None of these amount to a theory of truth, but they give us an idea of pre-philosophical reflection on truth which is consistent with our commonsense understanding of truth as a matching of our thoughts with the world.

Similar examples can be found in the Hebrew Bible or *Tanach* (*Torah, Neviim, Catvim*). For example, in the *Torah* (law), there is a very clear injunction against falsehood in the Ten Commandments. Leviticus 19:11 simply states, "Thou shall not lie" (Holy Bible 1993). If one were to formalize this using traditional categorical logic, the claim would be, "No things that you say are things that are lies." By obversion (changing the quality of the statement and replacing the predicate term with its term complement), the command would be, "All things that you say are things which are non-lies." This seems to amount to, "Tell the truth!"

In the *Neviim* (prophets) in the Hebrew Bible, there are references to truth, which have philosophical import. Biblical claims about truth in prophetic literature indicate the seriousness with which truth was valued by God, and what happened when things got really bad for those who were under God's judgment. For examples of various judgments on the nation of Israel, see Isaiah 59:14, "Truth has stumbled in the streets," Jeremiah 7:28, "Truth has perished," and Daniel 8:12, "Truth was thrown to the ground" (Holy Bible 1993). It seems that in each of these cases, the loss of truth serves as part of God's judgment. Truth was a serious matter and the loss of it in the life of the people a grave one.

In the wisdom literature, part of the *Catvim* (writings), one only has to look to Proverbs 23:23 to see God's emphasis on the value of truth. The wise one says, "Buy the truth and do not sell it" (Holy Bible 1993). Truth was something, along with wisdom, extremely valuable, much more so than worldly wealth.

It is safe to summarize the Hebrew Bible's view of truth as being a concept of something that is central to an ethical, moral life. It is a serious matter if truth is lost. Truth is something of great value to be treasured in one's life. These ideas played a central role in the nation of Israel's relationship to God. These ideas don't amount to a theory of the nature of truth as much as a moral commitment to truth, but at least in the commandment against falsehood, the emphasis is on talking faithfully about how things are. This is very similar to the ancient Greek concept of truth as accurately representing reality as it is, and is familiar to anyone who has experienced truth in the commonsense ways described at the beginning of Chapter 1.

2.3 Pre-Socratic Philosophy

While the ancient poems, laws, prophets, and wisdom literature present descriptions of truth, command the truth to be told, and place truth on a high moral plane, they do not give much in the way of philosophical reflection on truth. With the rise of philosophical reflection in Greece (often thought to begin with philosophers before Socrates), one has to look no farther than Parmenides.

One of the longer pre-Socratic reflections on truth is from Parmenides' fragments on truth (Kirk 1984). Parmenides neatly divides the philosopher's task of discerning what is properly called true knowledge from that which is mere opinion. It appears that Parmenides has two main tasks in this selection. First, he argues that there is a universal order of things that permeates all of reality. This is "the real" or "what is" or "being." The real is that which gives the cosmos its ordered nature, and its intelligibility. Second, after illustrating what "the real" is like, he considers the conjectures or opinions of the cosmos that are derived from an examination of "the real."

Parmenides' image is of the search for truth as a great journey which is "far from the steps of men". This is to say that the knowledge he has gained is not available to mundane thinking. Knowledge of "what is" is knowledge about things beyond the world of the five senses, and it is good to leave the physical to consider the metaphysical. Second, the purpose of his journey is to "learn all things" of which there are two parts. He is to learn "the unshaken heart of well rounded truth" and "the opinions of mortals, in which there is no true reliance" (Kirk 1984, p. 243). To know that which is true, and that which is false; to know fact from conjecture is Parmenides task.

Thus, Parmenides as a good philosopher moves from what he knows to what he does not know all the while building his case, but recognizing when he moves from fact to opinion. He knows that there is an essential being to the cosmos that pervades all things. He seems to recognize the rational ordering, of existence itself, and that being is not derived from nothing-ness. He also seems to recognize that mind is inherent in the nature of being, and that mind is different from matter. From this foundation he moves into that about which he is less certain, that is, the details of how the physical cosmos works.

It is Parmenides' real existing "being" that is the basis for all things, this is truly known. This knowledge provides one reason for examining the natural world. For on this account the natural world is full of the rational. The physical workings of the cosmos are ordered, understandable, and absolute, and able to be rationally and truly known. Truth then is fixed, permanent, one, and indivisible. In fact, it is too fixed. There can never be any change.

We can learn at least three things from Parmenides. First, the truth is out there. Truth seems to be something independent from us. Second, truth is different than opinion. Our ideas or beliefs may be held deeply by us, but they are true or false depending on something entirely distinct from what we believe. Finally, truth doesn't change. Our beliefs about what is true might change, but what is true does not. Again, Parmenides does not put these things in the form of argument or a philosophical treatise. What he does though, which differs from the literary and Biblical presentations of truth, is this: he considers truth as such from a rationally reflective point of view. Now, we have come to the philosophy of truth, which continues to the present day.

2.4 Socrates, Plato, and Aristotle

When Socrates was on trial for his life he made a big deal about truth and falsehood. Right from the beginning of his *Apology* he tells the jury both that his accusers have not told the truth, and that he will tell the truth. He does this knowing full well that it will get him killed. He even instructs the jury only to consider the truth of his words rather than his oratorical skill. Socrates' divine mission is to search after true wisdom. In considering the afterlife, Socrates delights in the possibility of an eternal "search into true and false knowledge; as in this world, so also in the next; and I shall find out who is wise, and who pretends to be wise, and is not" (Plato 1891). Socrates takes truth beyond mere truth telling and poetical use. He is concerned with truth philosophically in the sense that truth can be proven. Logical reflection, the use of reasoning, and rational evidence all play a part in Socrates' search for truth. One has to look no farther than the way in which Socrates defends himself against the accusations leveled against him in the *Apology*. He claims that he will speak the truth and make plain by reasoning that the charges of corrupting the youth and denying the gods are false ones. Socrates looks for truth. He devotes his life to it.

As a philosopher, his search involves the use of the intellect and reasoning toward the truth. Truth for Socrates is no different than it was presented in Homer or the Old Testament. It is still "telling it like it is." Truth is still conceived as an adequate representation of the way things are. Truth is still highly valuable for living. It is the only way to live as a human being. The unexamined life, a life without truth, is not worth living. Socrates brings to our understanding of truth something different than the poets, prophets, and law-givers. Socrates brings the intellect to bear on both the pursuit of truth and our consideration of what truth is. This is philosophy … a love of wisdom involving a life committed to intellectual reflection toward human well-being.

Socrates' student Plato follows his master in the philosophical love of the pursuit of truth. In his dialogues, Plato does not give a theory of truth with all of the technical details laid out in one place. Rather in several places in his works, he offers statements which rationally develop our understanding of what truth is. Plato presents a "philosophy of truth." Let us consider a few examples.

Plato indicates in the *Sophist* that truth is a quality of sentences. Sentences are true when they state facts as they are about some subject, and false when they state things that are not facts about some subject. For example, the sentence "Theatetus sits" is true and "Theatetus flies" is false because the latter "says things different from those that are" while the former speaks of things that are as they are (*Sophist* 263b, Plato 1997a, p. 287).

This statement in the *Sophist* doesn't seem much different than non-philosophical statements about truth expressing the way things are. Plato as a philosopher understands this idea of truth as a statement's correspondence to reality in light of his philosophical reflection, which does give a clearer account of how statements made by our intellects actually do or can correspond to reality.

For example, in the *Theatetus*, Socrates states that our opinions are true when they properly match up with our perceptions. This implies a kind of correspondence between one's opinion (or belief) and what one perceives. Socrates describes those who have false opinions as those who think of something, but cannot "have indistinct impressions [in the soul/mind]…they are slow and allot things to impresses which do not belong to them, misseeing, mishearing and misthinking most of them—and these in turn are the ones we describe as in error about the things that are ignorant" (Plato 1997b, p. 215, line 195a). Thus, Plato begins to develop an account of a correspondence view of truth by showing that there are two relata in the correspondence relation: the mind and the world. Truth can be a property instantiated in the match between these two.

Plato has additional philosophical reflection on truth in what I believe is his greatest work, *The Republic*. In his consideration of the qualities of a "philosopher-king," Plato indicates that a just ruler should have as part of their nature, "Truthfulness: they will never intentionally receive into their mind falsehood, which is their detestation, and they will love the truth" (Plato 1871, 486c). Plato, using an exchange between Socrates and Glaucon, elaborates on this view of truth stating that truth is similar to the concept of proportion. The proper ruler of the ideal city, which of course is analogous to the proper ruler of the soul, which is reason, must have the ability to be guided to the "ideal reality in all things" (486e).

When Plato says that our minds must conform to the ideal reality in all things, and that this is what truth amounts to, then we have here a great step forward in philosophical reflection about truth. For Plato, the most real things are the forms (universals or ideas) which exist in a transcendent, permanent, and unchanging reality. The forms can be present in the things which have them. For example, redness or roundness can be exemplified in a ball. To have knowledge, and ultimately truth about what redness or roundness are, we can look at the ball, but the ball can change, it can go flat or deflate, and the red color can fade. The truth about redness or roundness can be found when our minds truly see redness and roundness as they are as forms in an ideal reality. Truth thus can be had by the mind when it makes true judgments about reality: "The ball is red" is true just in case the ball is red. Yet, if we want to truly know what redness is, we can't just look at a particular red ball. We have to rationally abstract and see the property (universal or idea) of redness as it is in itself as a form or idea apart from the physical reality which exemplifies it. The great historian of philosophy Frederick Copleston explains that Plato's view of truth and knowledge involves knowledge of universals in such a way that "to each true universal concept there corresponds an objective reality" (Copleston 1993, vol. 1, p. 151).

For Plato truth is what it was thought to be by Socrates and by the prophets and poets before him: a correspondence of thought (belief) with reality (the way the world is). Plato takes this a bit further. Truth is present in the physical world, in our ordinary experiences of reality. Yet, the reality of truth in our ordinary experiences is itself due to a reality beyond those experiences. A belief becomes true because it has "proportion" with reality. My belief that a ball is round will be true insofar as what my belief is about conforms to the reality toward which it is directed. This is possible because of a reality beyond our experiences. The universals/ideas of "roundness" itself exist independently from the particular instances in which it occurs. My belief in a ball being round will be true insofar as I comprehend roundness as a universal (perfect roundness, like a perfect circle) and can use this knowledge of roundness to judge particular cases of roundness in order to see that the roundness of this particular ball matches or corresponds to true roundness. Let me make this explicit with another example.

Plato's main concern in the *Republic* is to arrive at an answer to the question, "What is justice?" So, he begins with various definitions of justice in Book 1. For example, "Justice is giving someone what is owed to them." This claim is shown to be false by giving obvious counterexamples which show that justice cannot be "giving what is owed to them." In other words, Plato shows that the claim "Justice is giving someone what is owed to them" is false; it does not correspond to reality any more than the claim "Theatetus flies" corresponds to reality. However, in order to arrive at the truth of what justice is, Plato using Socrates has to go in search of it. As the dialogue progresses, the truth of what justice is becomes clear. Justice in the soul consists in the proper parts of the soul fulfilling their functions in the proper way: reason wisely ruling in conjunction with the courage of the spirit (will) in order to moderate the body's desires. Now this definition of justice either corresponds to the way the world is, or it does not. The whole exercise of the *Republic* is to lead the reader to a place where she can see the correspondence of this ideal of justice to the reality which it is about, namely our own souls. Truth then is not only correspondence of our beliefs with sensory reality, but involves the connection of our beliefs with something higher than physical reality. Truth is thus itself a form, an idea, a universal which is both immanent in our experiences and transcendent from the empirical world as well.

Plato's reflections on truth in the *Republic* illustrate this dual nature of truth. Truth is present in our ordinary experiences, but understanding what truth is in those experiences requires reference to ultimate forms and ideas which transcend them. We will look at this idea further in Chapter 7 when we examine the correspondence theory of truth in the works of Edmund Husserl.

Plato's student Aristotle (384–322 B.C.) continues the line of philosophizing about truth along correspondence lines in his *Metaphysics*. This statement of truth by Aristotle is one of the clearest statements a correspondence view of truth in the history of philosophy. Here is what Aristotle says:

> This is clear [there cannot be an intermediate between contradictories] if we define what the true and the false are. To say of what is that it is not or of what is not that it is, is false, while to say of what is that it is, and of what is not that it is not, is true;

so that he who says of anything that it is or that it is not, will say either what is true or what is false; but neither what is nor what is not is said to be or not to be.

(*Metaphysics* Gamma (bk 4) ch. 7 1011b, p. 27)

There are several things to consider in this passage. First, notice that truth is bivalent. That is, there is truth and falsehood, and nothing in between. It is either one or the other. Second, the reason that truth is bivalent is that it is directly connected (if not almost identified) with being. Being is also "bivalent" in the sense that either something exists or it does not exist. There is no middle ground between being and non-being. Thus, truth is absolute; it *is* or *is not*. Third, and I think that this will be important for later linguistic approaches to truth, notice that Aristotle focuses on "what is said." One could infer from this that Aristotle only thinks that the bearers of truth are sentences or statements. That is to whatever extent truth is a matter of correspondence to reality, the things which correspond to reality are linguistic sorts of things. While it is possible that Aristotle could mean this exclusively, it would take a longer argument to demonstrate that either linguistic entities are the sole bearers of truth or that linguistic realities are not ontologically dependent on non-linguistic entities, such as thoughts or beliefs. In addition, I argued in Chapter 1 that truth cannot be linguistic. I take Aristotle's statement to be simply a bare bones framework which makes clear that truth in our statements that express our beliefs is always a matter of those beliefs accurately representing reality.

2.5 Medieval Christian philosophy

Greece waned. Rome waxed. Jesus was born in Bethlehem. Philosophical reflection on truth changed forever. Jesus is not often considered a philosopher, but his teachings on truth had a profound impact on the history of Western philosophy. This includes philosophical reflection on truth.

In the Gospel of John, the concept of truth and its connection with Jesus is drawn out right from the first chapter. Writing in a very philosophical, almost Platonic manner, the Apostle John says,

"The Word became flesh and made his dwelling among us. We have seen his glory, the glory of the One and Only, who came from the Father, full of grace and truth" (John 1:14). John is presenting the concept of truth in a radically different way than it has been conceived by previous philosophers. While truth is still a matter of the correspondence of reality to belief, and something of great value for moral living, it is here presented in personal form. Truth, literally an un-hiding or revealing, is present in the person of Jesus. In some ways the very idea of truth as a matching of a truth bearer and a truth maker (idea/belief/though with world/reality/being) is present in the very nature of Jesus. The New Testament authors including John connected all of reality to Jesus as the one in whom all things have their being. On this view, the truth maker side of the correspondence relation is dependent upon him. On the other side, the truth bearer is also dependent upon him: Jesus is the Word, the *logos*, of God. Jesus (as truth) is the word become flesh, the Son of the Father who perfectly corresponds to the way the Father is in bodily form.[1] This is also evident in John 14:6 when Jesus says, "I am the way the truth and the life." Jesus is certainly saying that he is the truth about the Father and the way to Him and eternal life in Him, but philosophers should inquire whether or not Jesus is saying something profound about his nature and the nature of truth itself.

It is the light of Christian revelation which provides the context for reflection on truth during what is called the medieval period. During this period, truth as correspondence was held and elaborated by many philosophers. St. Augustine (354–430 A.D.) maintained a kind of view of truth as correspondence. He states, "similitude is the mother of Truth" (Augustine 1910, p. 72). Augustine also says that, "truth is that by which that which is, is shown"[2] which indicates a relation between what exists (facts or things) and being "shown" (propositions). This can be understood as a correspondence view of truth.

Anselm of Canterbury (1033–1109 A.D.) held a version of truth as correspondence. He wrote, "A proposition is usually said to be correct and true when it signifies in accordance with that correctness and truth by which it affirms a thing to exist which does, in fact, exist" (Anselm 1967, p. 95). This is similar to Aristotle's generalization above. Robert Grosseteste (1170–1253) in his work *De Veritate* (*On Truth*) continued the tradition of truth as correspondence in his statement that truth of word or opinion is the adequation of the word or opinion and things (Copleston 1993, vol. II, p. 231).

Arguably it is with St. Thomas Aquinas (1225–1274) for which we have the most elaborate account, indeed a complete theory of truth that spells out in some detail how truth is the "adequation of thing and intellect." (Aquinas 1952, Question 1: Article 1, pp. 5–6). Aquinas expands Aristotle's account of truth by integrating Aristotle's metaphysical accounts of cognition and the nature of the soul with Aristotle's epistemology. We are able to say of something that is that it is because the soul takes in, in some way, the objects set before it.

Aquinas uses Aristotelian metaphysics to expand Aristotle's notion of truth into a form of the correspondence theory of truth in which truth is the adequation of thing and intellect. Later thinkers in the "silver age" of scholastic philosophy such as Francisco Suarez (1548–1617) also argued that truth is conformity between the understanding and things.[3]

One noteworthy modification of the notion of truth as correspondence is Aquinas' revision of one of Augustine's views of truth. Augustine held that "The true is that which is" (*Soliloquiorum libri duo*, II, 5). Aquinas revises this to "The true is that which is—it [truth] is had when the existence of what is is affirmed."[4] However, in one sense, Augustine's idea is less problematic than Aquinas' definition of truth as adequation of thing and intellect. Aquinas' definition can be modified slightly to capture what Augustine was after (i.e., a close identification of truth with being). The modified Thomistic reading of Augustine would be, "Truth is had by someone (but exists independently of someone) when someone's intellect is adequated with something."

2.6 Modern philosophy

In the "modern" era, Renee Descartes (1596–1650) apparently held to an internal account of correspondence. He speaks more of the "criterion" of truth more than he does a "definition" of truth. However, in his account of the criterion of truth, truth as correspondence is implied (Descartes 1988, p. 36). Descartes claims that one has to "see very clearly" the content of the proposition in order for the proposition to be true. This is, in one sense, an understanding of truth as correspondence between the proposition and the experience of an object, which is dependent on the object itself. At least for the "cogito" Descartes' understanding of truth is one of correspondence. Insofar as other truths are dependent on the kind of clarity and distinctness found in the cogito, Descartes' view of truth is one of correspondence.

Spinoza (1632–1677) also maintained a version of truth as correspondence. Although, an understanding of truth as correspondence is found in his account of knowledge, it can be extended to an account of truth in general. He maintains that there is a kind of knowledge that "proceeds from an adequate idea of the formal essence of certain attributes of God to an adequate knowledge of the essence of things" (Spinoza 1992, p. 90). The two things which, when in place yield a specific kind of knowledge, are one's idea of divine attributes and the essence of things. It seems that when there is a right relationship of correspondence between these two things, then knowledge and truth are present.

Spinoza was not the only rationalist who maintained a correspondence view of truth. Gottfried Leibniz (1646–1716) held to truth as correspondence as well. He stated, "truth consists in the correspondence of a proposition with reality, possible or actual" (Copleston 1993, vol. IV, p. 273).

On the empiricist side of the great Modern Divide, John Locke (1632–1704) also continued the tradition of truth as correspondence. In his *Essay Concerning Human Understanding* he states, "For *Truth or Falsehood*, being never without some *Affirmation, or Negation,* Express, or Tacit, it is not to be found, but where signs are joined or separated, according to the agreement, or disagreement, of the Things they stand for" (Locke 1975, p. 391). In another place in the *Essay* he claims that "Truth consists in putting together, or separating these Signs, according as the Things, which they stand for, agree or disagree" (p. 576).

David Hume (1711–1776) in his *Treatise of Human Nature*, while arguing that morality is not discoverable by reason, maintains that truth or falsehood consists in an agreement or disagreement of real relations of ideas, or real existences and matters of fact.[5] He claims that if anything is not susceptible to agreement/disagreement it cannot be true or false. This can be construed as a version of truth as correspondence theory of truth, where ideas and matters of fact are related in the right way to produce truth.

Marking the end of "modernity" and the beginning of "post modernity" Immanuel Kant (1724–1804), awakened by Hume from his dogmatism, continued the tradition of truth as correspondence. In his *Critique of Pure Reason*, Kant holds to a definition of truth as "the agreement of knowledge with its object" (Kant 1929, A 58, p. 97). He seems to accept rather than argue for the view that "truth consists in the agreement of knowledge with the object" (A 191, p. 220). In the "Appendix to the Transcendental Dialectic: The Regulative Employment of the Ideas of Pure Reason" he concludes, "the categories lead to truth, that is to the conformity of our concepts with the object" (A 642–643, p. 532). The main challenge for Kant is the "noumena-phenomena" divide. This is an oversimplification, but if the mind is never directly connected to the objects it experiences, then there is never really an "adequation of thing an intellect." There is an adequation of our concepts with the objects as they are experienced, but it is only an "internal" correspondence, but not a full adequation in the Thomistic or Platonic sense. It seems to me that all reflection about truth from Kant on will be plagued by this issue.

2.7 Post-Kantian philosophy

With the death of Kant, modernism had run its course. The empiricists' emphasis on experience as the guide of human life reached its fulfillment in Humean skepticism. The rationalists' emphasis on the internal workings of the intellect to reach for certainty lead to fantastic castles in the air. The major response to Kant's idealism was found in the great idealist thinkers of the nineteenth century. These thinkers simply bit the bullet of Kant's internalistic view of truth and extended it to include what idealists called the Absolute. All of reality as appearance is ideal, and truth along with it.

Georg Wilhelm Friedrich Hegel (1770–1831) makes truth to be the whole of a movement of the ideal as it unfolds within the absolute and not distinct from it. "The truth is the whole" of what is real, and the whole of what is real is the Absolute "reaching its completeness through the process of its own development" (Hegel 1949, p. 81). Truth is not "like a stamped coin" (p. 98) ready to be put to use. Truth has become something unfolding in an ideal reality, and not something fixed and external to our minds. Hegel collapses here the distinction between individual minds and external reality that might be truly known. The two are now one. The world that was fixed and distinct from a knowing subject who could come to experience the truth about that world has now been changed into an ideal unity of knowing subject and known object. The sober Aristotelian axiom that truth is a saying of what is that it is, and the realistic Thomistic notion of "adequation of thing and intellect" is replaced with the inebriated idealistic notion that truth is a "bacchanalian revel, where not a member is sober" (p. 105). Truth becomes something moving along with the unfolding of Absolute Ideal Reality. Hegel states, "Truth moves itself by its very nature; but the method just mentioned is a form of knowledge external to its material" (p. 106). We will examine more recent forms of idealism in Chapter 3 on coherence theories of truth.

There were of course exceptions to the dominance of idealism in the nineteenth century. One such example was the philosopher Bernard Bolzano (1781–1848). He maintained a fairly clear view of truth as correspondence echoing Aristotle when he wrote, "I shall mean by a truth in itself any proposition which states something as it is" (Bolzano 1932, p. 33). Another example in a more theological rather than philosophical vein was the Scottish novelist George MacDonald. In his "Unspoken Sermon" on "The Truth" MacDonald argues that while truth is a correspondence of mind to reality, it is much more than that. He claims that truth is intimately connected with God, echoing Jesus' divine claims to be the truth (MacDonald 1999, pp. 459-479).

There is a great deal more to a history of truth that is presented in this chapter. I have touched on a few highlights in the history of philosophy which do two things. I have tried to present a consistent line of thinking about truth as commonsense correspondence which is present in ancient literature, developed in the Greco-Christian tradition and into modernity. There have been challengers along the way such as Protagoras, Vico, and Nietzsche to name a few. However, the dominant view of truth in the history of philosophy has been some form of the correspondence theory. This does not entail that some version of the correspondence view of truth is correct; people can be mistaken for a very long time. It does however give one pause to remember that many far greater minds than ours, after reflecting about truth, have come to advocate some sort of correspondence view.

Beginning with Kant and through nineteenth-century idealism, this strong line of thinking about truth as correspondence has been majorly challenged. Hegelian idealistic notions of truth as being identical with reality and the knowing subject has played a good part in what has been called "coherence" theories of truth. We will dig a little deeper into idealistic thinking insofar as it applies to so called coherence theories of truth in the next chapter. Then, we will turn to other challenges to the traditional view of truth as correspondence which arose in part as response to idealism. These include pragmatism, linguistic approaches to correspondence, and deflationism.

3

Coherence

Chapter Outline

3.0 Introduction

I reach for my keys in my backpack to unlock my car. They are not there. I believe that I have left my keys on my desk. I return to my office (the secretary lets me in for the third time this semester), and I look on my desk. I see my keys. I swipe them off the desk, mumble my apologies again to the secretary, call my wife to let her know I'll be late (again), and head to my car.

When I experience a simple act of the adequation of my intellect and a thing, it always occurs in a particular context of other beliefs.

These beliefs might be very broad background beliefs about the nature of the world such as: things (like my car keys) don't regularly pop in and out of existence. My beliefs might be more narrow background beliefs such as, my memory is a fairly reliable guide to discovering where I may have put my keys. These beliefs are intricately connected with a whole host of other beliefs about what my keys look like, my belief that I was in a rush to leave my office, my belief that I had lent my keys to a student to open the copy room, my belief that the student had put the keys on my desk when they were done, my belief about the location of my office, the kindness and patience of our department secretary, and many others.

All of these beliefs are related to one another. When they are put together in an act of finding my keys to be as I thought them to be (an act of seeing the adequation of my intellect with things, *that is*, my keys) they form a reasonable whole. There is nothing particularly surprising about seeing my keys on my desk where I believe I left them. That belief is connected to the broad belief that things don't pop out of existence willy-nilly. That belief is connected also with the belief that my memory is reliable, that my office is still in the same place it always has been, and the secretary is as kind and patient as usual. We might even say that these beliefs all hang together in a coherent sort of way. They just go together. None of these beliefs are out of place, odd, or unusual, given my past experiences and the beliefs that have been formed by them.

Is this sort of coherence, the appropriate hanging together of our beliefs, what truth essentially consists in? It does not seem that it could. For the essential belief that is at concern here is: "My keys are on my desk." This belief coheres nicely with all my background beliefs, so I use it to go back to my office and look on my desk for my keys. Suppose that when I get to my office, I look at my desk, and see that my keys are not on my desk. I have a nicely coherent belief, "My keys are on my desk," but a false one. There is a lack of adequation of my intellect (my belief that my keys are on my desk) and things (my keys being on my desk).

So, I sit down in my chair to reflect on where my keys could be. I cannot think of any other place except one. I recall that a very clever former student who majored in philosophy and physics is now on a post-doctoral fellowship at MIT doing advance research on teleportation of inanimate objects. In our last e-mail exchange he said that they were not making much progress with the technology, but that he would make sure that he would let me know of any developments. At that moment, I form the belief that my keys are in a research lab on the other side of the country from California in Cambridge, Massachusetts. I video call my former student. He answers, and with a silly grin holds up my keys and says, "Looking for these?"

My belief that my keys are in an MIT lab doesn't cohere well with many of my other beliefs, but it turns out to be true. My keys were teleported across the country in an experiment which was broadcast live on the Internet during my afternoon class. When I formed the belief that my keys were in an MIT lab, that belief did not cohere with most of my other beliefs. It did, however, correspond with reality. This example gives us a reason to think that coherence among beliefs is neither necessary nor sufficient for truth. Coherence does not make sense of our ordinary experiences of truth, in a way that a correspondence view of truth does.[1]

While coherence has been thought to be central to truth, this chapter introduces a few different approaches to understanding the relationship between coherence and truth. These views of truth generally focus on the idea that truth is a matter of the coherence of one's beliefs, or truth is only possible when considered internally to various belief systems. In addition, while the approaches surveyed here vary in some of their details, what they have in common is a view of the nature of reality, a metaphysics or ontology, which is essentially constructivist. I mean by this term "constructivist" the idea that the world and things in it do not have the properties they have independently of our cognizing about the world. In one way or another, these approaches maintain that the world we experience does not have the characteristics that we experience apart from our experiences. I will try to make this explicit as we look at a few key figures, and I will offer a critique of this notion as we go along.

3.1 Idealist coherentism

3.1.1 F. H. Bradley

F. H. Bradley (1846–1924) was a British idealist who maintained an understanding of truth as coherence. His idea of coherence rests (as we will also see in the case of Brand Blanshard) on the idea of a "system" of beliefs in which we test our beliefs internal to a system "as wide and consistent as may be" (Bradley 1914, p. 202). This system is (and this will be a common theme for each of the coherentists we examine) itself constructed by our experiences. This system consists for us of our own world. Bradley sates, "We each of us have a world which we call our 'real' world in space and time" (p. 208).

Our systems are built to cohere by our experiences which become true "just so far as they work" (p. 201) within our constructed worlds. Truth becomes that which brings order to our constructed world system and becomes "a question of relative contribution to my known world order" (p. 211). Truth just is "that which enable us to order most coherently and comprehensively the data supplied by immediate experience and the intuitive judgments of perception" (p. 215).

There are at least two things to say about this view of truth. First, there is the question of the metaphysics that is behind the view of perception used by Bradley. He states explicitly, "There *is* a world of appearance and there *is* a sensuous curtain, and to seek to deny the presence of this or to identify it with reality is mistaken" (p. 218). Do we stand behind a curtain in our experiences? How do we know this? Would not this imply a regress? If all knowledge is curtained, then our knowledge of that is curtained, and our knowledge of that is curtained etc ....

Besides the issue of a regress, why should we think that there is a "blur" or a curtain or something that stands between us and the way the world is? This may be due to the fact that we experience *by means of* our sense experiences, but it does not entail that we experience *through* our experiences as if through a curtained window.[2] However, it is only through the latter view that it follows that our experiences and our perceptions are located (in the mind or brain or wherever) and thus that our perceptions are mediated (or curtained, to use Bradley's term). But there is no reason to think that our sense experiences should be understood in this latter way than in the former. We perceive or experience by means of our senses, but not through our senses. The error in selecting the latter instead of the former goes at least back to Kant's noumena/phenomena distinction and runs right through, without question, to the idealism of Hegel and Blanshard. It is beyond the scope of this work to offer a full defense of a direct (non-materialist) realist account of perception that is more reasonable than the indirect idealism assumed by Bradley here. This is a key point: Bradley assumes this metaphysics of perception which, I believe, must entail a sort of anti-realist version of truth as coherence.

A second worry for Bradley (and the other idealists here) is the issue of a coherent, but false "constructed reality." It is quite possible that one's perceptions are mistaken. One could (in theory if not in practice) manage to construct an entirely coherent world system from one's illusory experiences. This construct could be sufficiently broad enough to serve as a basis for action. It is possible that such a construct not adequately represent at all the world that it was supposedly about. (We will look at another issue with illusion in Section 3.2 below.)

3.1.2 *Bernard Bosanquet*

Bernard Bosanquet (1848–1923) also has a coherentist account of truth in his *Truth and Coherence* (Bosanquet 1911). Bosanquet's view shares the main feature of Bradley's coherentism. It relies on an idealist constructivist metaphysics. Bosanquet maintains that there is a Reality (capital "R" in his usage) beyond our experience. The world of our experience is still constructed by the mind. He states, "We construct our world as an interpretation which attempts to restore the unity, which the real has lost by our making its diversity explicit" (Bosanquet 1911, p. 5). Truth is thus understood as coherence within this constructed world system. This "thought world" is reality for us and the search for truth is simply the "endeavor to approximate as a system of ideas to a non-contradictory whole" (p. 10).

Sometimes Bosanquet talks of this coherence within a thought world as a test for truth (p. 13), but other times he speaks of this as a theory of truth (pp. 15 and 27).[3] What is clear is that Bosanquet rejects the idea that beliefs are true because they correspond to facts that are independent from our system of beliefs constructed by our experiences. He claims that facts are not "bits of reality immediately accessible to apprehension, and corresponding each to each with terms of our commonplace judgements" (p. 20).

Given our example at the beginning of this chapter, it is difficult to see why this could not be the case. We are at all times faced with clear cases of our thoughts matching things as they were thought to be. In such everyday acts, there is an implicit awareness of a direct, or what is usually disparagingly called naïve, realism about perception. These ordinary experiences seem to confirm rather than disconfirm a correspondence view of truth. My keys being on the desk was certainly not made by me, and my beliefs (when true) match the way the world is independently of my knowing it or not.

Bosanquet anticipates this sort of example of what he calls "stock-in-trade of daily life and conversation" (p. 22). In such cases, our everyday notion of fact consists of "the normal furniture of the world" (p. 22). Bosanquet denies that he is reducing facts to mental dependent entities, and even says that correspondence in this sort of commonsense view is fine as far as it goes. He admits that facts themselves are real but are "mediated to us by an immense mental construction, and are not really separate from this" (p. 25).

He is trying to convince his readers that this is only partially right. He gives the example of a historical fact "Charles the 1st died on the scaffold." He argues that such historical facts are less true when uttered by a schoolboy and more true when uttered by a history scholar. The scholar has a broader, wider, deeper "system" of thought in which this singly selected belief finds its place. Because the expert's belief (e.g. "Charles the 1st died on the scaffold.") is embedded in a more complex coherent system of beliefs, it is more true than a mere boy's belief.

I believe that Bosanquet is mistaken about this. Consider an example to the contrary. It surely is the case that a historical belief held by an expert rather than a non-expert will stand in more complex relations with other beliefs. We need to ask: How does this determine the truth of the belief?

One could maintain that the scholar and the schoolboy just live in different worlds. Truth in the scholar's world is more complex and rich than in the schoolboy's. Bosanquet actually seems to hold this, when he says that we each live in different worlds (p. 30). He says that all subject-predicate judgments are "relatively given" and are "in some degree different for every mind" (p. 31).

This is looking an awful lot like a combination of ontological and epistemological relativism. All judgments are made by some standard of evaluation, and there are no neutral standards (see Mosteller 2006). Since Bosanquet recognizes the relativity of these points of view (p. 31), it is difficult to see how his views will avoid the major problem with relativism. It is self-defeating.[4]

His idealism may be his way of avoiding relativism. According to Bosanquet, there is an Absolute Ideal Reality behind all of our judgments. This is the Reality behind the curtain of our experience. Yet one might ask, how is this known, and on what grounds is this thought to be true? If the world of appearances that we construct by means of our minds is "absolutely plastic" (p. 31), then how does one ground the truth of the belief in something beyond it? In addition, the claim of absolute plasticity is itself a subject-predicate judgment which either describes the way the world is apart from our knowledge of it, or it does not. If it does, then coherentism is given up. If it does not, then coherentism cannot be established. The idea that the world of our thought experiences is absolute plastic is itself absolutely plastic. This makes for a very incoherent view of coherence. We will examine a similar notion in Alcoff's more recent views of coherence below.

3.1.3 Brand Blanshard

Brand Blanshard in his *The Nature of Thought* (Blanshard 1939) develops his view of truth as coherence in a similar way to Bradley and Bosanquet. He denies the existence of mind independent facts to which our beliefs might correspond. Facts are, he insists, relative to the system in which judgments about them occur, and coherence is the only test of truth or fact (Blanshard, p. 215).[5] This again is an idealistic anti-realism in which our world is only known by means of constructed experiences.

Like Bosanquet, Blanshard anticipates commonsense realistic correspondences view of truth based upon our simple experiences of finding the world as we thought it to be.[6] Blanshard argues that in a simple case of perception, say of a cardinal in the tree, we do not perceive cardinals. We are perceiving "sense data." In other words, there is something which stands between us and the world: a sense datum (Bosanquet's curtain). According to Blanshard, all of our perceptions are theory laden, which means that they require judgments in order for us to have them, and are capable of error (p. 230). There is no simple perception for Blanshard.

I argued above in Section 3.1.1 on Bradley that this view only follows if sensory perception is understood as "through" the senses such that something like a sense datum stands between us and the objects we perceive. Yet, sense perception can be understood as "by means of the senses" which leaves no ontological blur between us and the world.[7] If the latter is possible, then Blanshard's view of facts fails.

Blanshard further criticizes a commonsense correspondence view. He argues that truth can't be a matter of correspondence because in any perception, it is possible to be mistaken. This can't be a serious objection to correspondence. If my belief matches reality, then my belief is true. It is possible that my belief doesn't match reality, but it does not follow that I am in error.

We need to distinguish here between truth being correspondence of belief to reality (adequacy of thing and intellect) versus our judgments about our beliefs corresponding to reality. My belief that my keys are on the desk, either matches the keys being on the desk or not. I can go look. In looking I can experience the matching of my belief with reality, and I can make a judgment about the relationship. The former can be true, my belief can match reality, and my judgment about that matching can be mistaken.

Think of it this way. Suppose I have a belief that my keys are on my desk. I go look, but when I turn on the light in my dark, windowless office, I happen to be looking right at the light when it turns on. This produces blurriness in my vision, so that when I look down at my desk, right in the spot where I believe my keys to be, I only see a blur of a light afterimage and brown color from the desktop. I'm in a hurry, so I flip the light off, and leave the office mumbling to myself about where else I could have left my keys. Now, in spite of my not seeing the keys on the desk, the keys are on the desk right where I left them. The belief is still true, even though my judgment about my belief being true is mistaken. There is a distinction between a belief being true and our judgment about our belief being true.

Blanshard continues his critique of correspondence by giving an illustration to show how correspondence is not a good test for truth. He gives two examples: one from ordinary perception, the other from logic. For his example from ordinary perception, he cites Sir William Crookes, a nineteenth-century chemist and physicist. In a scientific experiment, Crookes reportedly observed and photographed the reality of "spiritualist" activities produced by a "medium in a trance". These activities included the "materializations of disembodied spirits" (p. 235). Blanshard indicates that Crookes had a belief that there were disembodied spirits present in the experimentation room, and that his belief may have corresponded to reality. However, since they did not cohere with the established scientific views of the day, they were not counted as true. Blanshard concludes that we should not take the matching of our beliefs with our perceptions as conclusive for truth, but should only accept this "only if the consequences of rejecting generally the sort of evidence here presented would be intellectually more disastrous than those of accepting it. And this is the appeal to coherence" (p. 237).

This sort of example seems to confuse truth and justification. Surely, Crookes' belief could have been true in the commonsense view of correspondence. However, given great counterevidence from established scientific views, Crooke might lack justification for his belief such that his true belief could not be counted as knowledge.

For his example from logic, Blanshard maintains that logical laws do not correspond to any sort of extra-mental reality. Quoting C. I. Lewis, Blanshard writes, "Any current or accepted canon of inference must be pragmatically determined" (p. 250). It is here that the coherentist notion of "system" is crucial to understand. Logical "laws" according to Blanshard are only laws within or relative to a particular logical system.

While it may be possible to "construct" alternative logical systems (multivalued logics, "fuzzy logics" etc.), this does not necessitate the falsity of obvious logical truths, even of the Aristotelian variety. For example, "No S are P" and "Some S are P" are contradictory. One might ask, "In what possible world could they not be contradictory?" The former asserts that there is nothing in the S/P category overlap, and the latter asserts that there is. To assert both simultaneously and univocally would be to assert that something has being and does not have being. Logic and metaphysics here are intimately tied together. Even if it cohered within a system of belief that something could have being and not have being, there is no possible world in which that could be true. This is a necessary truth, the denial of which entails a logical contradiction on any possible logical construct. This is not so much a defense of truth as correspondence as it is to show that Blanshard's view of "truth relative" to a logical system is in need of revision. Several more recent attempts at revising coherence have been given, and to these we now turn.

3.2 Recent coherentism

3.2.1 Ralph Walker

Ralph Walker (1989) begins a defense of coherentism along similar lines as Bradley, Bosanquet, and Blanshard. Walker extends the approach to coherentism from the constructivist idealism of the early coherentists to a strong form of metaphysical (and epistemic) anti-realism. He is very clear to deny that truth consists in a "correspondence between the proposition and *some reality which obtains independent of anything that may be believed about it*" (p. 2). On Walker's coherence view of truth "the facts are themselves determined by the coherent system of beliefs" (p. 2).[8]

For Walker, facts are not independent of us. We make them. He states, "our standards of rationality and justification are...reliable guides to reality. For reality is what these standards make it" (p. 14). In other words, we make the standards. We create reality. Walker's ideas are a very long way from Aquinas' notion of the adequation of thing and intellect. If you reject the possibility of adequation of one's mind with a reality independent of one's mind, then you end up with pragmatic constructivism of the sort which Walker advocates. The world ceases to be something to which my mind conforms; rather the world is made by me.

According to Walker, truth cannot be "correspondence with independent reality" because reality is determined by our own classification through our beliefs. Therefore, truth is nothing but "some kind of internal coherence among our beliefs" (p. 16). From this idea, Walker gives an ontological argument for coherence to the conclusion that: "Our grasp of a concept like 'green' is not to be explained in terms of our latching on to an objective similarity among green things" (p. 17).

Here is his argument: "If there were such objective similarities, there is no way in which we could know about them, since we can be aware of things **only by** applying concepts to them and hence by classifying them in some way ourselves; so the objective similarities could play no part in governing our use of concepts" (p. 17). Here is a simplified (and clearer) sketch of the argument:

1. If we are aware of things (including similarities), then we use our concepts to create things.

2. We are aware of things (like "green").

3. Therefore, we use our concepts to create things.

4. If we use our concepts to create things, then there are no objective similarities.

5. Therefore, there are no objective similarities.

Unless someone is willing to deny that we have awareness of things, then the key premise to this argument is premise 1. This amounts to the idea that what we are aware of is conceptually constructed. This is ambiguous. The ambiguity lies in a distinction in the concept of "being aware of things." In any act of experience (what Walker calls an awareness), there are at least two things: (1) the thing that I am aware of, and (2) the awareness itself (and possibly the awareness of the awareness). Walker seems to conflate the thing I am aware of with the awareness itself. Of course, I can't be aware without an awareness, but I can be aware of a thing without being aware of the awareness itself.

Walker says that if we are aware of a thing, then we use our concepts to create that thing. If he means by "thing" here the awareness of an awareness of a thing, then of course, I can't be aware of an awareness without thinking about my awareness. In a minimal sense, awarenesses are "created" by the mind, in that they would not exist without the mind having them. Without the mind's capacities to be aware, awarenesses could not come into being.

However, it is absurd to maintain that being aware of a thing implies that the thing is created by a concept for at least two reasons. First, things (desks, people, cars) being what they are could not be produced (given their characteristics) by consciousness or language being what it is. Consciousness simply cannot do this sort of work on extra-mental reality.

Second, if things take their properties from language and/ or consciousness, this will be because, or due to what language and consciousness *are*.[9] This demonstrates the absurdity of any constructivist or anti-realist view of truth. Each of these views which we have examined here (Bradley, Bosanquet, Blanshard, Walker and Alcoff, as we shall see) maintain that somehow language or consciousness or the mind itself and thus truths about them are immune from the constructive tasks that shape reality. If the mind (language, consciousness, or whatever) does the constructing, then the mind itself is not constructed. Thus not all reality, and not all truths about that reality, are constructed. Thus, a coherence approach to truth which rests on such a metaphysics cannot give an exhaustive account of truth.

3.2.2 *Linda Alcoff*

Another recent coherence approach to truth comes from Linda Alcoff in her "A Case for Coherence" (Alcoff 2001). In that paper, Alcoff gives a summary defense of her ideas regarding truth developed in her longer work, *Real Knowing* (Alcoff 2008). Alcoff begins her case for coherence with a recognition that there are a multiplicity of truth claims which often appear contradictory. What was often thought to be true, has often turned out not to be true (p. 160). She claims that a coherence understanding of truth can make sense of this apparent puzzle, because coherence of beliefs are "mutually explanatory" coming from multiple avenues such as "inference, correlation, analogy, or even similarity" (p. 161).

We might call this "The Boy Who Cried Wolf" objection to truth as correspondence. When the boy in the fable keeps crying "Wolf!"

and there's no wolf, people just give up believing him. The boy is no longer believable. The same goes for people who maintain a correspondence view of truth, but are continually wrong. We ought to reject the approach to truth that is behind all of these false claims.

However, this simply does not follow. From the fact that the boy who cries wolf has false claims about wolves attacking the sheep, it doesn't follow that if there were a wolf that the claim that there is a wolf would not correspond to it. This simply means that the claims that are made that are claimed to be true simply don't correspond to reality. To accept a correspondence view of truth is not to maintain that every claim to truth is always correct. Some truth claims are false. Alcoff's motivation for a coherence over a correspondence view of truth appears misguided.

One of the interesting things about Alcoff's view of truth is that it clearly recognizes that coherence involves a rejection of a robust realism (as we have seen in Bradley, Bosanquet, and Blanshard). This involves denying at least three things: (1) that the world is independent from human knowers, (2) that the world would be as it is if there were no human knowers, and (3) that we can know the world as it is in itself. Her view of coherence rejects a clear distinction between the mind and the world, and between knowers and things known. She maintains that her view of coherence involves a rejection of what Dewey calls "the spectator theory of knowledge" and Adorno called "peephole metaphysics" (p. 162). Human knowledge is immanent in ontology, in reality. She states, "knowledge is ultimately a product of phenomena that are immanent to human belief systems and practices, social organizations and *lived* reality" (p. 163).

"Spectator theories of knowledge" and "peephole metaphysics" are, I believe, a result of accepting the Kantian distinction between *noumena* and *phenomena* as a result of a general loss of understanding the reality of "qualities" in both the physical world and the intentional aboutness of mental states which are the natural affinities of those qualities. To argue for this would require a long textual journey in the history of philosophy. But it seems to me that there is a clear slide from Gallileo's "tickled statues" to Kant's *noumena/phenomena* bifurcation. Once you remove qualities from the real world you end up with some sort of idealism, whether subjective/materialistic (Berkeley), transcendental (Kant), or absolute

(Hegel). So I agree that "spectators looking through peepholes" is the wrong metaphor to understand epistemology and ontology, but that is not the only alternative to anti-realism. Alcoff gives us a false dilemma: spectators/peepholes *or* anti-realistic coherence. There are other varieties of realistic options. Platonic, Aristotelian, Thomistic, or Husserlian realism is a viable option with fewer problems than the idealism mentioned here. Some of these options with respect to truth will be discussed in Chapters 7 and 8 on commonsense realism about truth.

It does no good to replace "spectator theories of knowledge" and "peephole metaphysics" with what Dallas Willard has called "Midas Touch" epistemologies (Willard 1993). King Midas needed only to touch what he wished to be gold, and gold it became. Alcoff's view that knowledge is produced by human belief systems, practice and social organizations recognizes that human action produces much of what is real. Yet to say that our knowledge of that reality is produced by human activity simply misses the point. It does not take into account the self-refuting nature of the claim. Human beliefs, practices, organizations, actions and language will all be able to do these things because they are determinate sorts of entities with determinant sets of properties which can putatively *do* the things that Midas Touch epistemologies say they can. Human beliefs, practices, organization, actions, and language are either conditioned themselves or not. If they are conditioned, then they must be conditioned by something else, and now we are off to the races with a bit of a regress. On the other hand, if they are unconditioned, then Midas Touch anti-realism fails, as there are things which exist with determinate properties apart from human practices, beliefs, organizations, or whatever.

The traditional concerns about coherence views of truth are addressed indirectly by Alcoff. First, there is the concern of equally "coherent" but contradictory systems of belief. Again, the objection is that they can both be coherently true even though logically contradictory. One way to resolve this situation is to relativize truth claims to standards of evaluation.

Alcoff does treat this type of relativism as a result of the "ontological pluralism" which she maintains. Alcoff rightly recognizes that relativism stems from the dual epistemic claims that (i) all epistemic judgments or truth claims are bound to particular standards of evaluation and (ii) there are no neutral standard to adjudicate a dispute among standards. The standard logical objection to this type of relativism is that it is self-defeating (Mosteller 2006, 2008). Alcoff does not consider this objection for relativism, but rejects relativism because it fails to offer reasons for "our need to revise one's own beliefs and practices in light of their differences from others" (p. 175).

The need to revise our beliefs and practices hinges on the notion of "revision" which can be understood by means of an analogy. When I follow directions on a map when I am trying to get to an unfamiliar place, sometimes I have to make revisions to my route toward the goal of getting home. Some revisions have to be made to take into account of the realities on the route. For instance, if there is a major accident on the highway, and the road is closed, my route will be revised to a detour around the closed road still directing me toward home. We might call this a "reality revision." Still, I might revise my route just for sheer pleasure, to take the scenic route up the coast and over the mountains. We might call this "personal preference revision." I might also extend the personal preference revision to radically alter my route by heading in a different direction altogether, and taking a road into a foreign country and simply declaring my home to be there. Call this *radical* personal preference revision.

Using this analogy, Alcoff might be considering reality revision, or personal preference revision. If the former, then this pulls against her anti-realism, and this is more akin to a correspondence rather than a coherence view of truth. If she means by revision something like personal preference revision, then she is still faced with the same problem of relativism. Why prefer one personal preference over another regardless of how radical? It's possible to have two radically different routes on a map that tell you two really different places about where your home is, but they point in opposite directions.

The second traditional objection to coherence is that it is possible to have an entirely coherent set of beliefs which does not match up with reality at all and are purely fictional. On Alcoff's view, the best view of truth is one in which there is an "achievement of coherence among the multiple and diverse elements involved in the process or flow of knowing practices" (p. 164). According to Alcoff, truth is "both plural and changeable, since it is relative to a context richly conceived" (p. 164). She adds that some contexts or "discourses" are so powerful that they "resonate in us and connect with other discourses, practice, or experiences, because they help us to make sense of something we have already experienced or because they are reinforced by other powerful ideas" (p. 166).

The problem of fully coherent but false beliefs applies here. Powerful ideas may resonate and connect with other powerful ideas in such a way that they motivate not only to have consistent beliefs but also to pursue a path of action based upon those consistent beliefs. However, there are clear examples of powerful discourses, and practices which when acted upon are disastrous for human living. The genocides of the twentieth century might be clear cases of this (Rummel 1997). This is not to say that genocides are a result of coherence theories of truth. It is simply to say that one can have a coherent powerful, resonating ideology which results in lots of dead people. Coherent belief systems can be false because they don't correspond to reality.

Let us turn to two final considerations of Alcoff's views. First, there is a quibble about the question over whether a commonsense understanding can apply to truth claims in other more complex domains. Alcoff seems to think that commonsense understandings of truth such as "There's a girl in your room, or there isn't" simply can't be applied to scientific questions like "Either electrons exist or not exist" because she believes that "When a claim is especially theory-laden, it is intuitively obvious that there is no simple fact of the matter" (p. 167).

There are two problems here. First, it is possible to make a claim like "there's a girl in your room" just as "theory-laden" as questions we have about electrons. Second, in both cases, finding out the truth is simply a matter of looking. It might be harder to find out what electrons are like than it is to find out whether there's a girl in my son's room. From this fact it doesn't follow that truth is not the same in each case. Truth can univocally be correspondence of intellect and reality regardless of the domain of inquiry.

Finally, on Alcoff's own view, her claims about truth being a matter of coherence are themselves unstable. Here are a couple of quotations from her essay. She states, "achieving coherence is never fixed or stable, and its very instability works to guard against facile or premature declarations of its achievement" (p. 179). She concludes with this: "Where the ultimate criterion is coherence within a large constellation of elements in a temporally and spatially specific context, rather than a foundation purportedly linked to truth outside of history, truth will always be temporary and unstable" (p. 181). The problem is that when the ideas in this quotation are applied to her own view of truth understood as coherence, then the truth claims made in her paper have not achieved any fixed or stable position. In fact, her truth claims are themselves unstable.

Alcoff could mean here that it is possible that her own position could be mistaken, or that it is not as coherent as it could be. Yet, if the coherence view that truth is unstable is itself unstable, and that claim is unstable, then, it looks like we've got an infinite regress of unstable claims. Everything will be unstable. How unstable? It seems difficult to figure that out if there is no fixed point or stable place to be.

At the same time, Alcoff's point here is instructive for those who maintain a correspondence view of truth. In her essay, from beginning to end, Alcoff is careful to remind us that truth claims can be mistaken. We may not always have the truth. What we think is true, may not be. This is a good point of wisdom going back to Socrates. The beginning of wisdom is a recognition that I do not know. We should have the sense to know that we don't know. It is true that we don't always have the truth. All theorists of truth and all philosophers, lovers of wisdom should recognize this point as valuable insight into our pursuit of truth. Yet, this seems only possible if there are truths to be known, and knowledge of truth which are stable, fixed and entirely independent of any putative coherent "flow" of human discourse.

3.2.3 Francis Dauer

The difficulties of coherentism are rather strong. The possibility of contradictory but coherent belief sets and the possibility of coherent but entirely unconnected to reality belief sets seem quite plausible. In addition, I have suggested that the coherentism of Bradley, Bosanquet, Blanshard, Walker, and Alcoff rests on untenable metaphysical and epistemological assumptions associated with a constructivist view of reality and our knowledge of it.

However, recent defenses of truth as coherence have attempted to get around these objections. One such response comes from Francis Dauer (1974). Dauer provides a "conditional defense" of the theory of coherentism based upon two key assumptions called V and M.

V: The truth or falsity of meaningful sentences makes a publicly observable or verifiable difference. (Dauer p. 791)

M: As a conceptual matter, if S is an observation sentence for us, a sentence S' of another linguistic community cannot be translated by (or mean the same thing as) S if S and S' have different stimulus meanings. (p. 792)

V is a verification principle and M is a semantic principle. Taken together, these assumptions are thought to be sufficient to answer the two main objections to truth as coherence: (a) that "several incompatible but equally coherent systems" could both be true, and (b) "that an entirely coherent system could be wholly false" (p. 793).

Dauer attempts to respond to (a) by limiting the concept of truth as coherence to "*actual* judgments or statements we make" (p. 794) rather than any possible set of propositions. These actual judgments are expressed as "observation statements" which are "stimulus-prompted utterances of, or assent or dissent to, an observation sentence by a particular speaker at a particular place and time" (p. 795). When two sets of observation statements conflict, the one which implies more observation statements and has more desirable characteristics of a theory is the most acceptable set (p. 796). He then moves to give a brief notion of competency of observers, where an observer is considered competent "until there are reasons to doubt them" (p. 796). From these two ideas it follows that "no statement and its negation can both have positive coherence" (p. 797), and thus, "there can't be two incompatible but equally coherent systems if this means that a statement and its negation can both have positive coherence" (p. 797).

The argument seems to amount to the idea that given the empirical, causal functioning of our noetic equipment in gaining observation statements which are derived from external stimuli, only those observation statements which cohere are going to be true for competent observers. Thus, if p is an observation statement grounded in experience of a competent observer, it already coheres with the subject's other observation statements. Thus, ~p will necessarily not cohere, and thus p and ~p cannot both have positive coherence.

This is question begging. The objection to coherence is not that if an already coherent statement is accepted because it is coherent, then the negation of that statement can also be accepted in a coherent system, especially if it is for one person. Suppose one person has a set of beliefs into which p coheres, and another equally coherent system into which ~p coheres, where p and ~p are equally plausible given his experiences. You could imagine a detective story or an abductive argument to the best explanation of a given hypothesis.

Suppose one investigates a crime scene and examines the evidence and in one list of evidence the observation statements entail a probability of n% that the maid committed the crime. Yet, on another list of evidence equally coherent within the overall context of the crime scene, equally derived observation statements fit into another coherent scheme in which the evidence entails the same probability of n% that the butler did it, which would logically entail (assuming that the butler and the maid are different people) ~p.

In such a case the observation sentences p and ~p could equally cohere in the noetic structure of an investigator. The evidence points with equal weight to the maid and to the butler. The statement p, The butler did it, and the claim ~p, The butler did not do it (because the maid did it), are contradictory, but each has positive coherence within the explanatory schema of the investigator's inferential abduction. Thus, Dauer is mistaken when he claims, "there can't be two incompatible but equally coherent systems if this means a statement [p: the maid did it] and its negation [~p: the maid did not do it] can both have positive coherence" (p. 797).

The second major objection usually leveled at coherence theories is that it is possible to have entirely coherent systems which are simply false in their totality. All the beliefs cohere with one another, but all the beliefs are false. Dauer responds to this by arguing that positive coherence is not "merely contingent" (p. 797). He argues that "the relation between truth and coherence" is an internal one. By internal, he means that there is a necessary connection between truth and positive coherence.

He first attempts to give a characterization of the group of competent speaker observers (G) which is not defined in terms of truth. This he does by claiming that membership in G is fulfilled by belonging "to the winning consensus when one's observation statement conflicts with others" (p. 798). If one is in G, then one will be in agreement with the majority consensus of other speaker-observers. Second, if there is a majority consensus agreement, then necessarily it is impossible for these observation statements to be false. Therefore, "T: The denial of 'The vast majority of observation statements are true' is conceptually impossible (or makes no sense as an empirical hypothesis)" (p. 799). The concept of truth is built into membership in G. Thus, for the members of G, it is conceptually impossible that most of the observation sentences be false. Thus, truth is not contingently, but necessarily related to coherence of observation statements within G.

There are I think at least two problems with this attempt to get out of the "Coherent but False" objection. First, there are problems with Dauer's ideas regarding what it means to be a member of G. While Dauer does not appeal to truth for membership in G, it still seems possible that the "winning consensus" can still get the world wrong. Perhaps there is a perceptual error, or perhaps there is intentional misreporting of observations. It is possible that a majority can still be mistaken. Further, why should one think that this characterization of membership in G is true itself? Even if it were defined in terms of coherence, it would only be true if the majority of speaker observers (professional philosophers, maybe) agree with it.

Second, there is a flaw with Dauer's attempt to make coherence necessarily internal to truth. Imagine a possible world where G has only one member. If there is only one member, then everything the member believes will be true. Perhaps one man with courage makes a majority, but in this case one man with an observational sentence makes truth. Thus, everything will be true in such a world.

This is absurd. But even if there were more observation statements for S than for not-S, it seems like the majority could just be wrong, say, in cases of mass hallucination or a simple observation of a bent stick in water. The majority of observers would claim, without further investigation that the observational sentence, a stick bends when placed in water is true based upon the normal stimuli response of simple observations that the stick appears bent when placed in water. This might cohere with the majority of competent observer speakers, but the sentence isn't true. The stick lacks the property of being bent. Thus there can be coherence with falsehood.

Dauer does consider a possible response to the problem of illusions in a footnote (p. 800), and claims that it is in principle possible to make room for this in his account. But I'm not sure how. It will always be logically possible that coherence among belief sets does not really reflect the way things are. This will not be a problem if one wants to maintain that truth and reality are determined by majority agreement based on stimuli generated observation statements. The world would thus be what we (the majority members of competent language users) say it is. This seems like a pretty crass form of anti-realism. Its crassness is logically untenable. The principles which begin the account of coherentism about truth must fit into the overall scheme of coherentism. But do they? Why should we think that the majority of competent language users agree with the starting points here? These seem like they are quite up for debate, and thus are not coherent within a group of competent language speakers, and thus are not true. Further, the principles for the argument for coherentism look an awful lot like they are telling us how things are apart from our consensus. This seems to give up coherentism. So either coherentism must be given up until everyone agrees with it, or if coherentism is even to begin it must be given up to tell us how things are.

In this section, I argued that one recent attempt to get around the traditional rejections of coherentism fails, and thus these objections stand. Even if my criticism of Dauer fails, there are at least three other problems for coherentism as such. In the next three sections, I will sketch these three challenges to coherentism.

3.3 Challenges to coherentism

3.3.1 Coherence entails probable falsehood

Peter Klein and Ted Warfield (1994) have a general argument against the truth conduciveness of coherence *as such*. The general idea is that necessarily any set of beliefs which is consistent has a specific probability of being true that is less than 1 and greater than 0. Yet, when you add any belief which is also less than 1 and greater than 0, even if that belief makes the set more coherent, necessarily the probability of the whole set being true is lowered. The more members of a set of beliefs, the less likely they are taken together to be true. The probability of the set of beliefs being true decreases as the set grows in number of beliefs.

This problem for coherentism focuses on the fact that somehow a mere group of coherent beliefs is supposed to be truth indicative. However, the argument demonstrates that the probability of truth is lowered as group membership increases. Thus, coherence can increase while the likelihood of truth decreases. Responses to this argument have been many. For a survey of various responses and counterresponses to Klein and Warfield's ideas, see Olsson (2012).

One possible response to Klein and Warfield is that their argument begs the question against the coherentism. When Klein and Warfield identify that the probability of "being true" lowers as the number of beliefs increase in a given set, they are presupposing "being true" to refer to truth understood as correspondence. However, the coherentist rejects this notion of being true. The coherentist maintains that truth just is coherence, not probably being true *qua* corresponding to reality. For Klein and Warfield, the notion of *being true* for just one belief means that there is a probability that it is true or false less than 1 and greater than 0. The coherentist can argue that if two beliefs cohere, there is nothing with respect to probability involved at all. Truth just is coherence. The probability of being true would not be pegged to corresponding to reality, but with the probability of coherence. But necessarily the probability that two beliefs *cohere* can't simply be measured by group membership. The question should be what the probability is that beliefs cohere and are thus made true given the increase in group membership. This recognition that the idea of truth presupposed in Klein and Warfield need not be accepted by the coherentist, since this is exactly what is in question is the nature of truth. This might make a coherentist view of truth immune from the kind of criticism raised by Klein and Warfield, but it does not deal with the internal incoherence of coherentism to which I now turn.

3.3.2 *Coherence and approximate truth*

Elijah Milgram offers a criticism of the very notion of coherence. He starts with a definition of coherence which begins with the idea that if someone is presented a decision about which ideas to include in a set of beliefs, there are both positive and negative constraints which tell you which idea should be in the set and which idea should be excluded. In addition, the constraints are weighted. He indicates that the task of these constraints "is to find a way of dividing up the set of elements, into an accepted set and a rejected set, which satisfies as many constraints as possible, taking due account of the relative importance of the constraints" (Milgram 2000, p. 84).

Milgram identifies this definition of coherence to a puzzle called MAX CUT. MAX CUT is the problem of how to figure out the maximum number of cuts which can divide up any particular graph. The bigger, more complex a graph gets, the greater the MAX CUT. Thus, it is impossible to figure out the MAX CUT for infinitely complex graphs. This is called "NP (nondeterministic polynomial)-complete" which means that they are practically insolvable in time, and can only be approximated. However, any approximation of coherence will always have a lot less in common with the most coherent account (which is impossible to compute).

So, Milgram advocates rejecting this idea of coherence as a way of getting at truth at the level of theory. It is simply impossible to put to practice. However, approximations are not a problem if your interests aren't in maximum coherence, but merely satisfaction of particular practical goals. Milgram advocates approximation of coherence to practical goals such as planning. Coherence approximations in the sense used/defined above, works really well with planning, because planning is relative to individual interests, and truth/correct beliefs are secondary. Coherence works when being coherent is relative to the practical interests of the believer.

What this indicates to me in a general reflection of the concept of coherence as it applies to truth is this: coherence as a general notion is impossible to obtain since it is NP complete. Since approximations are the only possible solution to determining coherence, and those approximations are determined by the interest of the individual considering a coherent system, coherence reduces to pragmatics.

What counts as a coherent approximation to idealized coherence is determined relative to the interests of the individual knower.

In his defense of his concept of coherence as constraint satisfaction, even for approximations, Paul Thagard (2012) leaves the very idea of constraint satisfaction open to the possibility of multiple constraints being applied to a coherence algorithmic probability calculation approximation. It seems that which constraint satisfaction requirements are chosen are again user interest based. This seems to reduce constraint satisfaction to pragmatic interests. This is fine as a general way of understanding the concept of coherence, but as a reduction of coherence to pragmatics, coherence will suffer from the problems of pragmatic accounts of truth which we will cover in Chapter 4.

3.3.3 *Coherence is incoherent*

Richard Fumerton offers a very persuasive criticism of the very concept of coherence. His argument is that coherence cannot make sense of the existence of relations and beliefs and maintain that truth is a matter of coherence. The main problem is that necessarily a coherentist theory of truth relativizes the beliefs which are held to be coherent to the individual. Not only does this imply the traditional problems with relativism (*viz*. that it is self-defeating), it also implies that coherence itself is always relativized to a system of beliefs.

Fumerton points out (1994, p. 94) that the problem is how to understand the *relata* of the coherence relation. Coherence is a relation of beliefs to one another in a coherent sort of way. A belief *P* will be true if it coheres with a set of beliefs *Q*. *Q* is true because it coheres with a set of beliefs *R*, and we are off to the races. Fumerton states, "The coherence theorist faces a fundamental conceptual regress" (p. 94).

Fumerton continues with an excellent summary of this problem of a coherence theory of truth when he says,

> We never get an account we can understand of what makes it true that someone has a certain belief. But without an account of what makes it true that someone has a belief, we don't have an

account of what makes any proposition true, because the theory attempts to understand the truth of the other propositions in terms of the *truth* of propositions describing a coherence between a proposition and other propositions *believed*

(p. 95).

Fumerton's critique is devastating for an account of understanding truth as coherence. It demonstrates that because coherentism relativizes true beliefs to coherent relations among beliefs, coherentism is internally inconsistent. One cannot say that truth is a matter of coherence without saying something true about the *relata* of coherence and the nature of the coherence relation itself. Fumerton points out that any attempt to do so on a coherentist view will necessarily appeal to the relation of coherence. These relativizing aspects of coherentism indicate that reality is radically conditioned by our beliefs such that truth become a matter internal to a belief dependent reality or coherentism is reducible to what is useful in the way of belief relative to an individual believer (pragmatism). I have argued against anti-realism throughout this chapter, and I will argue against pragmatic approaches to truth in the next.

3.4 Conclusion

In this chapter, we have examined several major approaches to truth which can be labeled coherence based. We have seen that many of these approaches rely on anti-realist or constructivist metaphysics and epistemologies. I have provided a few critiques of these approaches. These critiques have given reasons to doubt whether the very idea of coherence as applied to truth can do much beyond giving us some indication that our beliefs when true are usually coherent with other things we believe. This isn't much, but it does give us pause to realize that our commonsense experiences of truth are usually coherent events in light of our experiences. Truth can be surprising and may call into question the very coherence of all of our beliefs, but still remains a matter of the adequation of our intellects and things.

4

Pragmatism

4.0 Introduction

I reach for my keys in my backpack to unlock my car. They are not there. I believe that I have left my keys on my desk. I return to my office (the secretary lets me in for the third time this semester), and I look on my desk. I see my keys. I swipe them off the desk, mumble my apologies again to the secretary, call my wife to let her know I'll be late (again), and head to my car. The ability to see that one's belief is true is independent of our desires that our beliefs be true. It is possible to will strongly that my keys be or not be on my desk.

My keys being on my desk and the matching of my keys being on my desk with my belief that they are on my desk are independent of all interests or desires which I may have. However, the reality of the matching of my belief with the way things are may fulfill my interests (or not). The fulfillment of our intellects by things in the world does allow us to act. The experience of truth has pragmatic implications, but is independent of pragmatic interests. It is much easier to unlock one's car if one has the truth about the location of one's keys, but the will and actions which flow from it can be engaged apart from it. In American pragmatic philosophy that spans the nineteenth and twentieth and twenty-first centuries, there is a shift away from correspondence as traditionally understood as the "adequation of thing and intellect" to a view emphasizing the potential experiential consequences of a proposition's being true and the pragmatic use of language. In this chapter, we will look at two classical pragmatists (C. S. Peirce and William James) and one recent pragmatist thinker (Robert Brandom).

4.1 Classic pragmatism

4.1.1 C. S. Peirce[1]

C. S. Peirce (1839–1914) endorses that truth is a form of correspondence of world to thought. He did not think that this view of truth was wrong. He maintained that it is at the wrong grade of clearness. Peirce held that there were three grades of clearness for ideas. At the first grade of clearness, one can use a term competently. At the second grade of clearness, one can give a verbal definition (give an adequate account of the term with other terms). At the third grade of clearness, one can give a term's pragmatic meaning (i.e., its potential experiential consequences). Peirce claimed that truth understood as correspondence was merely a verbal definition, but it lacked pragmatic meaning in this third sense. Peirce emphasizes the difference that truth makes in our experiences. He states, "The opinion which is fated to be ultimately agreed to by all who investigates what we mean by truth, and the object represented in this opinion is the real" (Thayer 1982, p. 97).[2] This is still a form of truth as correspondence, but there is a shift to include the opinions, the practical experiential consequences of investigators or inquirers that is somewhat absent from earlier notions of truth as correspondence.[3] This movement to include the experiences of inquirers develops more fully in later pragmatic philosophy until the notion of truth as correspondence becomes largely a relation between the desires of individuals and the world which is created by individuals.[4]

Peirce's rich account of truth is grounded upon his pragmatic maxim. This maxim is the pragmatist's "tool for improving inquiry" (Olshewsky 1983, p. 200). Peirce develops the maxim as an alternative to Descartes' notion of "clarity and distinctness" as the criterion of meaningfulness. In this section, we will look at three things. First, the purpose of Peirce's pragmatic maxim will be disambiguated. Second, the actual experiences by means of which Peirce grounds the maxim will be stated as examined. Third, a general worry about the scope of the pragmatic maxim as a tool for inquiring into the meaning of all concepts will be raised.

The purposes of Peirce's pragmatic maxim as applied to meaning or truth, is simply to provide a "rule about meaning" or truth (Olshewsky 1983, p. 200). The pragmatic maxim must be understood not as a theory of anything, but rather as a formulation of a methodology of inquiry. This methodology is used to separate meaningful from un-meaningful metaphysical (and other) claims, and explain which concepts are in fact meaningful.

One of the clearest formulations of the pragmatic maxim is found in Peirce's "How to Make Our Ideas Clear." Peirce's central project in this paper is "to formulate the method of attaining to a more perfect clearness of thought" (Thayer 1982, p. 81). The state of clarity Peirce is after is not what he calls the first grade of clarity wherein one can merely use a term competently, nor a second grade of clarity wherein one can give a verbal definition of a term (i.e., give an adequate account of the term with other terms). Rather, Peirce is after what he calls a third grade of clarity which is where one is able to give a term's pragmatic meaning which, we shall see, amounts to the term's potential experiential consequences.

There is an initial ambiguity which needs to be clarified about the purpose of the maxim in "How to Make Our Ideas Clear." Peirce's statement that he is trying to attain "to a more perfect clearness of thought" or make "our ideas clear" (p. 82) is ambiguous between:

i.   the clarity of the idea as it appears to the one having the idea (i.e., the awareness of the idea qua idea), and

ii. the clarity of the idea itself as a clear *representation of* (or having a clear *fit with*, or *correspondence to*) the predicates of mind independent objects that it is thought to be an idea of.

It would be odd if Peirce were seeking to make our ideas clear exclusively in sense (i). Arguably, it is the nature of an idea to be immediately present to one having the idea. Ideas present themselves in such a way that one could not be unclear as to what the ideas themselves are. If I were asked to state my idea of the landscape of the city of Los Angeles and I indicate that there are a few small quaint Alpine buildings nestled in a lush mountain valley with a clear brook flowing through it, this idea would be clear in sense (i) and unclear in sense (ii). It would be clear in sense (i) since it appears directly to me, and I am directly aware of its contents since I use it to describe the properties I think Los Angeles to have. (I am appeared to "Los Angelesly" when asked to state my idea of Los Angeles. From this appearance, I state my idea.) However, my idea of Los Angeles is unclear in sense (ii). It does not give a clear representation of the properties of the mind independent object (Los Angeles) which the idea is about. If Peirce means by "making ideas clear" that one's awareness of one's ideas can be unclear, then he is open to the objection that the nature of ideas is such that one cannot be mistaken (and have false beliefs) about what those ideas are about.

Peirce appears really to want to make ideas clear in sense (ii). When he states how one reaches the third grade of clarity, he indicates that he is after a "clearness of apprehension" (p. 88) where apprehension can be understood to mean the grasping of the object that one's concepts (literally "grasp withs") are of. That Peirce is after clearness in sense (ii) is also evident when he says, "It is certainly important to know how to make our ideas clear, but they may be ever so clear without being true" (pp. 99–100). He recognizes the distinction between an idea being clear in sense (ii) (i.e., one's awareness of the idea itself), while at the same time being false (i.e., not corresponding to the world). It is by means of the pragmatic maxim that Peirce wants to clarify one's awareness of the fit between one's idea and the object that the idea is of.

The clarity of our ideas by means of the pragmatic maxim for Peirce is based upon the actual experiences of inquirers. The following are the three types of experiences to which Peirce appeals as the grounds or warrant for the maxim:

(1) the experience of the relation of thought to belief,

(2) the experience of the connection of belief to habit, and

(3) the experience of the connection of habit to meaning.

The first experience upon which Peirce grounds the pragmatic maxim is the experience of the relation of thought to the production of belief. He states that the "sole motive, idea, and function [of thought] is to produce belief," (p. 85) and that "the soul and meaning of thought ... can never be made to direct itself toward anything but the production of belief" (p. 85). While, for Peirce, the final purpose of thought is action, the first step toward action is the generation of a belief. Beliefs are produced in the process of thought producing action. He states,

> Thought is essentially an action. The *final* upshot of thinking is the exercise of volition, and of this thought no longer forms a part; but belief is only a stadium of mental action, an effect upon our nature due to thought, which will influence future thinking. (p. 85)

Peirce indicates here that we can simply experience the connection of thought with belief especially when thought produces action through belief.

The second experience which Peirce indicates as warranting the pragmatic maxim is the connection of belief with the establishment of habit. He states, "The essence of belief is the establishment of a habit, and different beliefs are distinguished by the different modes of action to which they give rise" (p. 85). Peirce identifies belief with a disposition or tendency to act in a certain way. A belief is the belief it is because it specifies a tendency to act in a specific way. Two beliefs differ in virtue of their different tendencies to action. He states, "The whole function of thought is to produce habits of action" (p. 87). We experience thought's production of habits through beliefs. Thus, there is a connection with what is thought to experiencable consequences of what is thought (i.e., habits).

Peirce's third experiential warrant for the pragmatic maxim is found in the connection of habit with meaning. Peirce indicates that the determination of the meaning of an experienced sensation is found in the habit that the sensation produces. Peirce states, "To develop its [a sensation's] meaning, we have, therefore simply to determine what habits it involves" (p. 87). Thus, when a sensation produces an idea, if one wants to know what the meaning of the idea produced by that sensation, one need only to look at the habit that the sensation produces.[5] Peirce appeals to the actual experiences that people have to establish this idea.

If the meaning of a sensation, or the meaning of an idea produced by a sensation, is determinable by looking at the habit it produces, Peirce effectively presents an example of how the meaning of ideas in general can be determined. He states, "Thus, we come down to what is tangible and practical as the root of every real distinction of thought, no matter how subtle it may be; and there is no distinction of meaning so fine as to consist in anything but a possible difference of practice" (p. 88).

In "Pragmatism and the Normative Sciences" Peirce examines the meaning of "practical consequences" and offers a proof that "the possible practical consequences of a concept constitute the sum total of the concept" (Peirce 1935, 5.27: p. 21). This proof is another indication of how Peirce, by appealing to one's experiences of the connection of habit with meaning, shows how the meaning of ideas in general can be determined. The proof is stated as follows:

i.   Belief consists in being deliberately prepared to adopt the formula believed in as the guide to action (p. 21).

ii. Therefore, "The proposition believed can itself be nothing but a maxim of conduct" (p. 21).

This argument identifies belief with a disposition to act on the content of belief. By connecting thought to belief, belief to habit, and habit to meaning, Peirce has presented, based on what one in fact experiences, that if one wants to get to the meaning of one's ideas, one must go through an examination of the habits that those thoughts produce. He has made a connection between the mind/ thought and the world. If one wants to determine what one's ideas mean, or if one's ideas have a meaning at all, or if there is any "real distinction" between the subtleties of different ideas, one need only to look at what is "tangible and practical" in the habits that those thoughts produce.

Peirce summarizes his three-part experiential warrant for the pragmatic maxim as follows:

> our action has exclusive reference to what affects the senses, [1] our habit has the same bearing as our action, [2] our belief the same as our habit, and our [3] conception the same as our belief; and consequently we can mean nothing by [any concept (wine in this case)] but what has certain effects direct or indirect upon our senses
>
> (Thayer 1982, p. 88)[6]

Peirce further states that having an idea is nothing more than our idea of its sensible effects on an inquirer. He states, "Our idea of anything *is* our idea of its sensible effects" (p. 88). The intermediary between ideas or concept is the habits that are produced by beliefs. Peirce states, "It is absurd to say that thought has any meaning unrelated to its only function [the establishment of habit]" (p. 88). This concludes his presentation of the three types of experiences which lead one to see the pragmatic maxim at work. Let us turn now to Peirce's explicit statement of the pragmatic maxim.

In "How to Make Our Ideas Clear" he states the pragmatic maxim for making one's ideas clear as follows:

> The rule of attaining the third grade of clearness of apprehension is as follows: consider what effects which might conceivably have **practical** bearings we conceive the object of our conception to have. Then, our conception of these effects is the whole of our conception of the object (p. 88). [emphasis added]

He presents the maxim in this way in "Pragmatism and the Normative Sciences":

> Pragmatism is the principle that every theoretical judgment expressible in a sentence in the indicative mood is a confused form of thought **whose only meaning, if it has any, lies in its tendency to enforce a corresponding practical maxim** expressible as a conditional sentence having its apodosis in the imperative mood [emphasis added]
>
> (Peirce 1935, 5.18: p. 15)

The key phrase in this formulation of the maxim that makes it similar to the one above it is, "meaning...lies in tendency to enforce a corresponding practical maxim." The practical effect of a concept or idea is what is essential in both formulations. However, the latter formulation is significantly different in its emphasis on the conditionality or the subjunctive mood. Here, the meaningfulness of an idea or theoretical judgment is found in the *possible* experiencable consequences of it. In both formulations, it is clear that Peirce connects ideas with their experiential consequences, and this is the heart of the pragmatic maxim as a method for improving inquiry.

One general concern for Peirce's overall conception of how one can determine the meaning of one's concepts is the distinction between "simple" meaning and "actualized" meaning. Simple meaning can be taken to be what the concept or idea is of even if what answers to that concept does not have existence. Actualized meaning can be taken to be the actual match, fit, or correspondence of some object in the world with what the concept is of. It seems that one can know the simple meaning of one's concept without knowing the actualized meaning (i.e., without ever experiencing what the concept is of). Peirce's statement of the maxim in the subjunctive supposedly alleviates this worry, but does it?

There are concepts which are such that they could not possibly have potentially **sensible** experiential consequences. Such concepts might include the concept that one is now aware of the thought of what Barack Obama looks like, or the concept of what it is like for one to see yellow. Peirce emphasizes the need for sensible experiences. He states, "Our idea of anything *is* our idea of its sensible effects" (Thayer, p. 88), and "Consequently we can mean nothing by wine [or any concept] but what has certain effects direct or indirect upon our senses" (p. 88). This worry could be alleviated for some concepts (like one's concept of what it is like for one to see yellow) if Peirce does not limit "sensible" to simply what is experienced through the five senses.

However, there is a further worry. Perhaps there are concepts that could not have any experiential consequences at all. These might include concepts like there is a mind independent world, or all of one's senses are reliable. It seems that experiential consequences may just have no bearing at all on how the meanings of these concepts are determined. As a tool of inquiry, perhaps the pragmatic maxim is only successful in determining the method of those concepts or ideas which actually could have practical experiential consequences. If there are in fact such concepts which have simple meaning but could not have actualized meaning, then the pragmatic maxim will only be useful as a tool of inquiry into the meaning of those concepts, and thus fail in an account of truth.

With this idea of the pragmatic maxim in mind, we can now turn to an account of Peirce's view of truth. Peirce defines truth as the opinion that would be agreed upon were inquiry pursued indefinitely (long enough). In "How to Make Our Ideas Clear" he states, "The opinion which is fated to be ultimately agreed to by all who investigate, is what we mean by the truth, and the object represented in this opinion is the real" (Thayer, p. 97).

There is an element of what Peirce says here that is similar to the commonsense correspondence view defended in this book. Peirce does maintain that the real is independent of what you or I or anyone thinks it to be. However, there is also an idealistic strain here as Peirce maintains that the real is the object of the final opinion, that is, what would be believed by the community of inquirers if inquiry went on long enough. This is often called "ideal-realism."[7]

These two distinct notions about reality are in tension with one another. On the one hand, truth is independent of what *anyone* thinks. On the other hand, the accessibility of truth seems dependent upon human inquiry. If Peirce makes truth too realistic, then there is a sacrifice of accessibility. We cannot know the truth of what we cannot practically obtain, given the pragmatic maxim of meaning. However, given the idealism which Peirce introduces, there is "group mentality" involved, which keeps truth from being independent of thought in general. We saw this as a major problem in the idealistic philosophies of truth as coherence as well as the constructivist anti-realism of recent coherence theories (see Chapter 3).

Peirce attempts to relieve this tension in "How to Make Our Ideas Clear." This is often called "The problem of buried secrets."[8] This arises concerning propositions about the past or which are such that no amount of inquiry can settle the truth of them. Susan Haack gives an example similar to the following proposition: "There are exactly *n* number of whiskers on the first cat in Los Angeles" (Haack 2004, p. 419). Certainly there was a first cat, in Los Angeles, but coming to find this out might be difficult, if not impossible. In other words, all one has to do is present a proposition which is meaningful, but lacks any pragmatic value, that is, cannot be experienced in the sense discussed above concerning Peirce's view of the pragmatic maxim. No matter how long or how many people inquired about such a proposition, we could never say if it is true or false. But, certainly such propositions are either true or false, but they might not be settled however long the enquiry lasted. If Peirce were right about this, then either such propositions don't have truth value, or truth is something other than what we achieve at the end of inquiry.

Peirce's pragmatic view of truth then has these two major difficulties. First, there is the problem of Peirce's ideal realism. Again to quote from Peirce, at the end of inquiry "the object of the final opinion depends on what that opinion is" (Thayer, p. 97). There is some ambiguity here. On the one hand, Peirce could mean that what is real "the object" about which we have our opinions, depends for its existence and its properties on what we (or future inquirers, or all inquirers together) think. This seems absurd. How could something now buried take not only its existence, but its existence as the kind of thing that it is from inquiring minds? While "Inquiring Minds Want to Know" (as the old *National Enquirer* slogan went), "inquiring minds" don't create or sustain in existence the things about which they inquire. This is another example of the Midas Touch Epistemology at work. Peirce could mean, however, the object of the final inquiry is nothing more than what is *believed* about the object being inquired about. However, this seems to make truth nothing more than a function of belief, and makes truth something epistemic, perhaps as a matter of coherence of a group of inquirers. This too seems to sacrifice the independence of truth.

The last major difficulty for Peirce (and for all pragmatists) is that there is the question of the pragmatic maxim itself, or a pragmatic theory of truth itself. Does such a theory really tell us about the way truth is? If so, then it depends on truth as correspondence. If not, then it cannot tell us the way things are, and rests upon volition rather than the intellect. This, in broad Platonic psychological terms, makes the intellect a slave to the passions.

4.1.2 William James[9]

William James (1842–1910) wrote, "The pivotal part of my book named *Pragmatism* is its account of the relations called 'truth' which may obtain between our idea (opinion, belief, statement, or what not) and its object" (Copleston 1993, vol. VI, p. 335). James does not deny truth as a correspondence of ideas to reality.[10] He claims, like Peirce, that it is true but inadequate; it is weak on "pragmatic" meaning. James writes,

> Ordinary epistemology contents itself with the vague statement that the ideas must "correspond" or "agree"; the pragmatist insist on being more concrete, and asks what such "agreement" may mean in detail. He finds first that the ideas must point to or lead towards *that* reality and no other, and then that the pointings and leadings must yield satisfaction as their result. So far the pragmatist is hardly less abstract than the ordinary slouchy epistemologist; but as he defines himself further, he grows more concrete.
>
> (James 1968, p. 191)

Again, this passage doesn't deny truth as a correspondence with reality. It simply maintains that a "correspondence" view is weak on pragmatic meaning.[11]

With James, truth becomes more nominalistic, more particular (see Yong and Haack 2010). According to Susan Haack, "James distinguishes between abstract Truth and concrete truths" (Haack 2004, p. 419). The pragmatist maintains that absolute truth is "an ideal set of formulations towards which all opinions may in the long run of experience be expected to converge" (James 1909, pp. 266–267) as enquiry proceeds. This is a subtle but important shift from Peirce. Peirce indicates that truth is what *would* be the case, rather than simply what will converge. This is concept of something much more abstract rather than a concept of something particular and concrete as found in James.[12]

Truths in the concrete, or concrete truths (plural), are particular, specified, and verified propositions. This presupposes the notion of abstract truth, without which you cannot specify what is verified. However, it ties verification too tightly with truth. It is possible to have something be confirmed and false. If something is unverified, it would on this view be false. Truth in this sense is *made* and not discovered.[13] This may also be a conflation of verification (showing something to be true) and confirmation (showing something to be likely or probable). James might offer a rejoinder to this type of objection by saying that we have to hold that concrete truths are not necessarily true, but what is taken for true *now*. The response to this type of rejoinder would be to point out that the notion of concrete truths can't take hold without objective, non-pragmatic (in the Jamesian sense) truth. James uses the notion of non-pragmatic (commonsense correspondence) to get up to the idea of pragmatism and then kicks the ladder down. He lets go of a theory of *truth* and ends up with "confirmed propositions *at a time*" or a theory of "truth."

There are things which James says about truth that are true in one sense, but false in another. James maintains that truth is verifiable and leads successfully. He claims that true beliefs are good, and that truth pays. There's something right about this. A belief does aim at truth. Given the content of a belief as an intentional state directed toward a possible object, a belief has within itself the potentiality of its fulfillment with the object which it is about. When I believe *p*, I believe that *p* is true. Truth and belief are internally linked in this sense. True beliefs can be instrumentally valuable. While this is not to say that all true beliefs are instrumentally valuable, they certainly *can* be. It is easier to find my car keys if I start with a true belief than with a false one.

As Susan Haack has pointed out, James was criticized for believing that "whatever it suits you to believe *is* true" (Haack 2006, p. 33).[14] For example, James says things such as beliefs pay, and truth is what is satisfactory in the way of beliefs. There are lots of beliefs, especially in the area of ethics which can be understood as really helpful to get what I want, but are completely false. They might have a "high cash value" but violate a natural moral law.[15] While James may not have intended his view to lead to a kind of subjectivism about truth, it is possible that it can be interpreted it that way.

One of the things which pragmatism does teach about truth, including James' version of pragmatism, is that there are some truths which depend for their existence on my *actions*. Such a view is not inconsistent with a correspondence view of truth. It simply recognizes that in order for my beliefs to correspond to specific truths, my will must be engaged. The paradigm case for this is, I believe, in the realm of interpersonal relationships. It cannot be true that I am friends with Greg if I do not act according to my belief that we are friends. It is the action upon my belief that we are friends that creates the existence of the relation of friendship. William James' famous essay "The Will to Believe" is an excellent example of this type of view of truth. Defenders of a correspondence view of truth must remember that some truths can only come into existence by means of our volitional attitudes.

4.2 New pragmatism: Robert Brandom

We turn now to a recent pragmatic view of truth held by Robert Brandom. This view takes insights from traditional pragmatism and fuses them with ideas in analytic philosophy of language. Brandom's view of truth can be summarized this way: "What is important in the end is not what 'true' means, but how language works" (Brandom 1988, p. 92).

Brandom argues that the use of words like "true" or "false" are reducible to the practices of language speakers. We can call this project "linguistic-pragmatic reductionism." "Truth" is reduced to practical language use. In his carefully argued paper, "Towards an Analytic Pragmatism" (Brandom 2008). Brandom indicates that this project is consistent with an epistemology (a broad view of knowledge) which is empirical (knowledge is only from the senses) and an ontology which is naturalistic (the only things which exist are physical things).

Brandom begins with epistemological empiricism and ontological naturalism. He proceeds to do away with the commonsense idea of truth as a matter of correspondence of beliefs with reality. He reduces truth to the pragmatic functioning of shared language use. This whole process is nothing more than a physical occurrence.

He begins similarly to Peirce with meaning of words (with semantics) and argues for the pragmatic idea that words in a vocabulary mean what they do because of how the words are used. He calls this "semantic pragmatism." It is "the view that the only explanation there could be for how a given *meaning* gets associated with a vocabulary is to be found in the *use* of that vocabulary" (Brandom 2008, p. 7). This is a starting point upon which to build an account of how more simple vocabularies can say what must be done in order to accomplish something in a more complex vocabulary. A simple vocabulary which lacks a concept of truth could say what someone would have to do in order to use a concept of truth. Or to put it another way "although normative vocabulary is not *reducible to* naturalistic vocabulary, it might still be possible to *say* in wholly naturalistic vocabulary what one must *do* in order to be *using* normative vocabulary" (p. 9). This is the project of beginning with an understanding of semantics and moving to an account of truth. It is important to distinguish his view of semantics, of meanings as well as his account of truth.[16] I believe that the latter follows from the former.

His account of truth is prosentential. The word "true" will function analogously to a pronoun in ordinary grammar. For example, in a sentence like "What Francisco said is true," the word "true" functions like a "pronoun" "he" in the sentence "He is tall." "He" like "true" refers back to something else. "He" refers back to the person under discussion, and "true" refers back to a sentence that was uttered by an original speaker. Thus, "is true" is a "pro-sentence" in a similar way that "he" is a pro-noun. The word "true" functions "anaphorically."[17]

Brandom indicates that this anaphoric account explains how "ordinary remarks about what is true and what is false" should be understood. The commonsense view of truth and reference such as correspondence (e.g., adequation of thing and intellect) is "philosopher's fictions, generated by grammatical misunderstandings" (Brandom 1994, pp. 323–324). Instead of understanding truth claims as expressing a direct phenomenal awareness of the way the world is such that one's intellect is adequated (or corresponds) to the world, truth claims should be understood "as adopting a normative attitude—that is, endorsing the claim and so acknowledging a commitment. This attitude is presupposed by the possibility of ascribing an objective property and is not to be explained in terms of it" (p. 324). Brandom's approach to truth turns the commonsense notion of truth as adequation completely around. Instead of the mind conforming to the world, the world conforms to the mind understood in terms of the social practices of commitments, entitlements, and reasons. Yet, according to Brandom, there is no "loss of the world" because discursive practices are not "unconstrained by how things actually are" (p. 333). What is given up is a "picture of how things are as contrasting with what we can say and think" (p. 333). If "how things are" does not contrast with "what we can say and think" this entails that "how things are" is at least sometimes no different from "what we say and think."

In a recent introduction and defense of his prosentential theory of truth, Brandom states, "The prosentential theory of truth offers a complete, adequate, and satisfactory account of the use of the term 'true'" (Brandom 2009, p. 164). He explains that the way in which terms like "true" function is that they "inherit their contents from their antecedents" (p. 165), and that the "prosentential relation is one of content-*inheritance*: one must *already* have a good grip on the notion of the content that is inherited in order to understand it" (p. 165).

There is an initial worry here. If one has a good grip on the notion of the content that is inherited in order to understand it, then one has antecedent concept of truth. For one sees the content of one's belief or thought matching with the reality it is about. The word "true" may very well function in a pronomial or prosentential way in language use, but the original connection and relation between thought and reality is what the word "true" picks out. It does so because of our phenomenal awareness of it. It does so in the same way the word "red" picks out the property of red because of our phenomenal awareness of redness. The fact that there is content which is about the world and ultimately related to it is what makes the relation of truth *qua* adequation of thing and intellect possible. The word "true" and its function in language are secondary to the reality of truth itself.

This is impossible of course if it is impossible to have a direct, unmediated connection with things, with reality. Of course, on Brandom's view it does fail. Brandom follows what he believes to be one of Kant's "epoch-making insights" which is the "recognition of the *primacy of the propositional*" by means of which we make judgments. "Judgments are fundamental" according to Kant and Brandom. The challenge here is twofold. First, on a Kantian epistemology or metaphysics, which begins with judgments by means of propositional content, the mind is constructing the reality that it judges. We never get to the things themselves. We are cut off. We are outside the world as it is. There is no direct connection to reality beyond the propositional judgments we make. To repeat Brandom's phrase above, there is no contrast between the way things are and what we can say and think.

Yet, the worry remains. This "Midas Touch" fails to notice that if judgments by means of propositions are fundamental, it is because of what they are independently of judgments and propositions. This is so because there is a contrast between the way things are and what we can say and think. If Brandom's claim is true, then the Kantian *blur* between mind and world must be false; we do have direct access to these things as they are.

Let us return to the idea of "content" here which is central to the prosentential view of truth as anaphoric. Brandom does not understand content here in terms of referential intentional properties which have a phenomenal "aboutness" as their essential nature. Brandom understands propositional content "in terms of *inference* rather than *truth*" (p. 166). He starts with the Fregean idea that "two claims have the same conceptual content iff [if and only if] they have the same inferential role" (p. 167). He identifies conceptual content in terms of its *role* in reasoning. He states, "To be *propositionally* contentful is to be able to play the role both of *premise* and of *conclusion* in an inference" (pp. 167–168). This, following Frege, relegates "truth to inference" (p. 168). Brandom states, we can "pick out declarative *sentences*, as the linguistic items that express *propositions*, in terms of their role in *inference*" (p. 168).

There is a twofold problem here. First, there is a self-referential problem. Is the claim "truth is relegated to inference" true or false? If it is true because of its role in inference, then the claim is circular, or perhaps redundant and therefore isn't saying anything. If it is true because it corresponds because of its content to the world of inference and logic, then the claim must be given up. Not all content is relegated to inference. Second, there is a problem of how we "pick out" declarative sentences. We do this because of the propositional content we have about them, apart from the role that they play in inference. Propositional content is logically necessarily antecedent to logical inference and not identical to it. If we have direct access to the world, if we can see snow is white and from this form the proposition that snow is white such that the direct awareness of the phenomena in unmediated experience of the world as it is in itself, then propositional content is associated with propositions expressible in logic and expressed by means of language. This is impossible if one assumes a Kantian, Midas Touch epistemology.

Brandom further identifies content with pragmatic functioning. When we are "understanding a sentence, associating a propositional content with it" we have "practical mastery of its inferential role." This is, according to Brandom, a "kind of know *how* rather than knowing *that*." Really understanding propositional content is "a practical ability, a kind of skill: sorting possible inference into good ones and bad ones" (p. 169).

Brandom makes clear that propositional content identified with "know how" is not merely stimuli response. For example, when it comes to propositional content with statements such as "That is red," he maintains that a parrot doesn't get the concept of red just my merely squawking "Rwak—that's red." A photocell that causes a light to flash on and off does not understand "red" just because it is causally connected to the presence of red objects. We sapient beings get the concept of red, according to Brandom, because we

have the practical ability to sort inferences in which it appears as a premise or conclusion into good ones and bad ones, *your* response "That's red" ...is the making of *move* in a language game, the staking of a claim, the taking of a stand that commits you to such claims, precludes some other, and could be justified by still others. (p. 170)

He continues, "having practical mastery of that inferentially articulated space—What Wilfred Sellars calls 'the space of reasons'—is what *understanding* the concepts *red* and *wet* consists in" (p. 170). He adds, "understanding *is* that practical mastery" (p. 173). (This identification of conceptual content, especially of "red" will be refuted below.)

Brandom's "prosentential" view of truth requires semantic content. Semantic content is explained in terms of the functional role of reasoning as a practical skill (know how). This entails that truth is expressive and not explanatory. [18] This is a way of saying in one vocabulary, a naturalistic *qua* social practice of practical mastery of conceptual content, what one is doing when one uses normative epistemological truth talk. Truth is reducible to social pragmatics.

Another way in which Brandom shows how to say in a naturalistic vocabulary what one must be doing in order to be using normative epistemological vocabularies like truth comes from examples from computer programming (Brandom 2008). He claims that we can begin with a simple case of the use of a purely syntactical sense of a vocabulary, and moves to the idea of "what it is to *deploy* such a vocabulary, and what it is to *specify* practices-or-abilities sufficient to deploy one" (p. 12). He creates a simple "machine" which he calls the "Laughing Santa Automaton." This machine is able to "read" and "write" the vocabulary to process simple strings of syntax. It consists of a simple program which tells the automaton to construct only licit strings of combinations of the vocabulary set {h, o, a, !} such that you end up with some combination of "ho!" or "ha!" such as "hohoha!" or "hahohaha!" etc.

The point of this example is to show that a simple machine can deploy a vocabulary and read and write it in this "purely syntactic sense" (p. 14). Brandom then provides a graphic illustration of the simple programming of such a machine. The graphic illustration, he claims, is a "pragmatically mediated" way of specifying the abilities of the machine to read and write its vocabulary. In other words, he has given us a way to *say* in one vocabulary what one must *do* in order to be *using* another vocabulary. This will then be applied, with more complex changes to a way of saying in a naturalistic vocabulary what one must be doing in order to be using normative epistemological vocabularies like truth talk (and other normative vocabularies like ethics and esthetics).

4.3 Objections to Brandom's pragmatism

I would like to raise four general criticisms of this approach of semantic pragmatic reductionism. First, I will raise a general worry about the antecedent nature of meaning. Second, I want to raise an objection to the example from computer programming, which I will call the "Unused, User" objection. Third, I want to raise an objection using the insights from John Searle's now famous "Chinese Room" thought experiment. Fourth, I will consider a form of critique from Frank Jackson's "Knowledge Argument." Finally, I will consider how the normativity of truth pulls against Brandom's general account of truth.

4.3.1 Use presupposes meaning

I am worried that the very starting point of Brandom's argument is flawed. His line of reasoning contains ideas which presuppose meaning apart from the use of words. For example, there is in Brandom's discussion, the idea of a *discursive* practice. Without antecedent meaning apart from discursive practices, how does one distinguish a discursive from a non-discursive series of events?

Here are two sets of events: Set 1 {the rotating of the earth on its axis, the waving of tree branches in the wind, the yawning of a cat on the hood of a car} and set 2 {a student's act of thought exemplifying *modus ponens*, a debate between scholars about totalitarianism in Orwell's *1984*, an article claiming that there is sentient life on Mars}. How is it possible, on Brandom's view to pick out which set contains discursive practices and which does not? If each set were, according to a strong reductionist or materialist ontology, nothing more than physical events, then *qua* physical events, there would be nothing to distinguish them at all. Without an antecedent concept of *distinguishing* and *discursive*, which comes from something other than the physical world, there can be no ability to distinguish discursive activities in the physical world. There must be some meaning antecedent to an act of identifying a discursive event.

In addition, there are several concepts which Brandom can only use because of antecedent meaning. For example, he writes of vocabularies which can *specify*, *say*, and *count*. It does not seem possible that acts of *specifying*, *saying*, and *counting* can even be identified without intentional states of the mind which can see them as such. Thus, contrary to Brandom, meaning is presupposed antecedently to use.

4.3.2 *The unused user*

Brandom's argument from computer programming begins with the notion of a machine deploying a vocabulary, where "vocabulary" is understood in a purely syntactic sense. My objection here centers on the nature of "syntax." Brandom seems to believe that an alphabet as such can be understood in a syntactic sense, where the alphabet itself literally has no meaning. However, the distinction between two sets of physical markings, one set syntactical and the other non-syntactical, requires a concept of meaning from the outset. An immaterial mind with the power to assign meaning to physical markings is required for the existence of syntax. The very idea of syntax presupposes antecedent meaning.

One could claim that one set of syntactical markings is given meaning by another, but this simply begs the question of *whether* meaning is derived by one set of physical markings upon another. Even more problematic is the claim that one set of physical markings can *confer* the property of being syntactical presupposes the meaning of the one making the claim that there is *syntactical* meaning in the relationship between the set of physical markings.

In addition, one can imagine a possible world with only one set of physical markings which lacks the property of syntax. This shows that being syntax is separable from the physical markings which are assigned meaning as syntactical markings. Furthermore, one can imagine a possible world in which there are two sets of syntactical markings where one set supposedly gives the property of being syntax to the other set. However, this seems absurd. For one set of physical marks has no power to generate syntactical meaning without a mind making sense of or giving meaning to the interaction of the sets of physical markings. To conceive of a possible world where syntax is present, just is to use the mind to give meaning to physical markings to make them syntactical by using antecedent meaning conceived by the mind.

Finally, in addition to the reality that syntax requires antecedent meaning derived from a mind, the very notion that Brandom desires to defend by his pragmatic example (meaning = use) presupposes a user. Now, if it were true that meaning could be reducible to use, I would argue that there can be no use without antecedent meaning. The very notion of "use" requires antecedent thought and meaning. How does one distinguish the use of something from its non-use, especially of physical objects? Consider farmer Wilbur who is getting ready to start digging a new garden with a new shovel. Wilbur's neighbor Leo has just stopped by to watch Wilbur use his new shovel. All of a sudden, a strong wind, a near tornado, rips through the garden and Wilbur is caught in it with his shovel and is spun round and round with the shovel waving in the air striking wildly against trees, the soil, and his tractor. Leo sees this, and thinks, "Wilbur's got a funny way of usin' that new shovel." But is Wilbur *using* the shovel at all? No! He is simply being spun round and round by the wind. He does stand in a physical relationship with the shovel, which might be identical (or indiscernible) from the act of using the shovel to shovel. Leo's assessment of the situation is mistaken, because *using* is dependent on the meaning of the act which is determined by the intention of the actor *doing the using*.

4.3.3 A "Chinese Room" objection

Let us turn now to a second worry for Brandom's pragmatism. John Searle's famous "Chinese Room" argument (Searle 1980) was meant to show that someone could be locked in a room and fed Chinese symbols through the door and by using a key inside the room gives correct answers to the questions that were asked. However, this person would not know Chinese. There would be nothing meaningful to the act of answering the question, because meaning cannot be purely syntactical.[19]

I believe that this line of criticism applies to Brandom's reasoning in the computational examples that he gives. Using one vocabulary to *say* what one must *do* in order to be *using* a second vocabulary could be exemplified by someone who has no concept of whether she is "using" a vocabulary, or "saying" anything about "doing" something at all. The Chinese Room image of someone simply responding to stimuli in a "pre-programmed" fashion would not count as "saying" anything. It is simply stimuli response with the presupposition in the initial programming of meaning embedded to the observers outside the room. Thus, there can be "appropriate responses" without any meaning, or with meaning only built into the system from outside. Therefore, meaning cannot be reduced to use.

4.3.4 A "Knowledge Argument" objection

Because Brandom seeks to ground his prosentential account of truth on semantic conceptual content, and identifies content with pragmatic "know how," his view is susceptible to the same problems faced by functionalist accounts of the mind. Namely, it is possible to have perfect "know how" and still lack conceptual content normally understood as phenomenal awareness. This objection comes from Frank Jackson's knowledge argument. The argument begins with the idea that it would be possible for a blind neuroscientist to know everything there is to know about "redness" from a "third person" perspective (see Jackson 1982 and 1986). One could know in detail all of the conditions under which redness occurs in the motion of external bodies, wavelength of light transmitted to the eye, the brain states that occur when someone is "appeared to redly" or has an experience of red. A scientist could know all of that, but still lack knowledge of what it is like to see or experience red. If such a scientist suddenly gained her sight, she would have new knowledge of the phenomenal quality of redness which she lacked before gaining her sight. One point of this thought experiment is to show that one could understand everything from a third person perspective, but lack first person knowledge of redness. This shows that a complete description of the physically necessary conditions for experiencing redness leaves out what redness actually is.

Suppose Brandom's account of truth is correct. Here is a summary of his view:

> Pragmatism in the stereotypical sense [being true = taking true] becomes relevant when one conjoins the ideas of a performative analysis of taking-true, of the relevant performance as undertaking a personal commitment, and of the commitment as specifying the appropriate role of a claim in action-orienting deliberation, with the further idea that the measure of the correctness of the stance undertaken by a truth-attributor is the success of the actions it guides (Brandom 1988, p. 79).

Here is a more formalized summary of his view. For any proposition, p, p's being true or the truth of p is the following:

1. p being taken to be true, or believed by S

2. the act of performance of S's taking p to be true

3. the act of S's committing to p being true

4. the specification of the role of the linguistic claim made by S "p is true" performs in deliberation

5. the measure of success that 1–4 give to S's actions.

Suppose that we were to be able to give an exhaustive account of 1–5. Suppose we had a perfectly accurate account of what it is for someone to believe, perform, commit, use language, and respond to stimuli in "successful" action. Even if one had 1–5, something would be left out: the phenomena of non-linguistic, non-performative, non-physical direct awareness of one's thoughts matching the world as it was thought to be. Just as a blind neuroscientist with exhaustive knowledge of the physical antecedents to experiencing red would lack knowledge of redness, so too someone with exhaustive knowledge of 1–5 (a perfect pragmatic-linguistic-performative-grammatical knowledge) of the use of "true" would not know what truth is. [20]

One could respond to this objection in a way that Brandom anticipates and is used by classical pragmatists. This is another instance of the "Midas Touch" epistemology. This is to say that the world is made by our experiences. The problem again is twofold. Things outside consciousness cannot take their properties from consciousness. Second, if consciousness did construct the world, it would be because of what consciousness is. Nothing could be structured, unless something was unstructured.

Another way of looking at this line of objection is that to claim that 1–5 is the nature of truth is to claim that the world, independent of how we take it, *is* (corresponds to) as 1–5 present it. There is the irreducible, inescapable, intentional phenomenon of the content of 1–5 and an awareness of 1–5 matching with the way things are. Thus, if 1–5 were true, it would entail that 1–5 were false. The claim that truth is nothing but how language works would be true because it corresponded to the world of language use, and not because of how language works. Thus, the attempt to ground a prosentential theory of truth by means of reducing propositional semantic content to pragmatic functioning fails.

4.3.5 *The normativity of truth*

Connecting truth to anything pragmatic (whether semantics or personal preference) seems to pull against the normativity of truth apart from pragmatic considerations. This especially seems to be the case of logical truths. There is a normativity to logical truths that impinges upon both thought and action. Suppose one could give a reasonable pragmatic reduction of truth to language use. Consider two arguments:

Argument 1
  i. If P then Q.
  ii. P.
  iii. Therefore, Q.

Argument 2
  i′. If P then Q.
  ii′. Q.
  iii′. Therefore, P.

Consider two truth claims about Argument 1 and Argument 2.

T1: Argument 1 is valid and we are reasonable to believe it.

T2: Argument 2 is valid and we are reasonable to believe it.

Suppose that we could create two language games or two computer programs whose practices and use of language could consistently assert T1 or T2.[21] So language game L1 would consistently assert T1 and language game L2 would consistently assert T2. Which language game would be more reasonable? Remember that the truth that A1 is valid, and the truth that A2 is valid is determined by the linguistic use of the terms "is true" internal to that language game, as well as the truth of i–iii and i'–iii'. Suppose further that both L1 and L2 give "successful" leading to the users of L1 and L2. How does one choose which language game is more reasonable? Are we really willing to say that the fallacy of affirming the consequent is nothing more than a rule in a particular language game and that it is equally reasonable to *modus ponens*? This seems absurd. There is normativity to logic that is independent from language games and language use.

Traditional Aristotelian logic (especially Venn diagrams that represent categorical claims) can demonstrate this more clearly. Simply consider the relation of contradiction between the following categorical claims.

E: No S are P

I: Some S are P.

Consider then the logical claims (the relationship of contradiction) about the relationship between I and E claim.

C1: If an E is true, then I is false

C2: If an I claim is true, then E is false.

Suppose that we could create a language game such that the relationship between "Some S are P" and "No S are P" is programmed to always read "true." This would produce two new logical claims about that relationship to read:

C1*: If I is true, then an E is true.

C2*: If an E is true, then I is true.

Can a pragmatic-linguistic reduction of truth be accomplished in such a case? The answer is clearly no. This does not have to do with the impossibility of creating such a language game or even living in one. It has to do with the nature of I and E claims. I and E claims assert something about the nature of reality. They assert something about being and non-being. What is impossible to *do* in language is to eliminate the real distinction of being and non-being. C1* and C2* both assert that something "is" and "is not" simultaneously. This notion claims to eliminate the distinction between existence and non-existence by the very act of existence. This is absurd. Thus, any attempt to reduce truth to language use will fail, as truth as well as language as such rests on what is real and independent of language itself. In the end, it is more important to see what truth is, rather than know how language is used.

4.4 Conclusion

This concludes our discussion of pragmatism. I have presented an overview of classical and one newer version of pragmatism. I have also presented several objections to each type of pragmatism. Pragmatism as a movement is much broader than the views presented here. It represents an approach to truth and philosophy which takes into account the truth that practical results and the use of language are important for human life. Its main difficulties lie in confusion about how truth exemplifies itself in our ordinary experiences apart from the practical consequences and the use of language that accompany them.

5

Deflationism

5.0 Introduction

I reach for my keys in my backpack to unlock my car. They are not there. I believe that I have left my keys on my desk. I return to my office (the secretary lets me in for the third time this semester), and I look on my desk. I see my keys. I swipe them off the desk, mumble my apologies again to the secretary, call my wife to let her know I'll be late (again), and head to my car. When I see that my keys are on my desk where I had believed them to be, I see the correspondence of my belief with reality. I see my belief is true.

I had the belief that my keys are on my desk, which can be expressed by the proposition, "My keys are on my desk." I might even mumble to myself, "My keys are on my desk." Since I was teaching an introduction to propositional logic that afternoon, I might even call what I just mumbled to myself, p. Before I go look on my desk for my keys, I might even mumble to myself, "p is true." I start to wonder, what's the difference between mumbling "p" and mumbling "p is true." Don't "My keys are on my desk" and "It's true that my keys are on my desk" say the same thing? I wonder whether the proposition "It's true that my keys are on my desk" can be *deflated* to the proposition "My keys are on my desk" without any loss of meaning. Now I'm worried whether the very concept of truth is an "inflated" concept. I'm wondering whether the word "true" is redundant when added to an assertion. Any assertion with the locution "is true" can be deflated to more simple concepts like the assertion of propositions themselves: "*p* is true" can be deflated to "*p*."

In this chapter, we will examine two different approaches to what has come to be called "deflationism" about truth. Deflationism can be thought of as an alternative account of truth to coherence, pragmatism, or correspondence. It can also be thought of as a replacement for any "inflated" account of truth. We begin by examining a few arguments from Gottlob Frege which have influenced a more recent version of deflationism from Paul Horwich.

5.1 Frege

Gottlob Frege's paper "The Thought" (Frege 1956) begins with a discussion of the word "true." One of the aims in this paper is to show that "true" when applied to sentences should not be understood as a matter of correspondence between an idea and the world. In addition, Frege argues that the word "true" does not add anything to a sentence that is asserted. The two sentences, "*p*" and "it is true that *p*" have the same content, according to Frege. Whether or not Frege intended these arguments to serve as a basis for "deflating" the concept of truth, it seems that the conclusions of these arguments are used by other philosophers, such as Horwich, in arguing for deflationism. In this section, we will examine Frege's arguments to the conclusions that (1) truth cannot be understood as correspondence between reality and the intellect, and (2) that "true" when added to an assertion does not add anything to the thought expressed by the assertion.

Frege's paper has three arguments to the conclusion that "the attempt to explain truth as correspondence collapses" (Frege 1956, p. 291). His arguments are as follows:

Argument 1 (A1):

P 1.1: If two things correspond perfectly, then they are identical.

P 1.2: The correspondence theory maintains that the two things that correspond are reality and the intellect which are not identical.

C1: Therefore, two things cannot correspond perfectly.

Argument 2 (A2):

P 2.1: If two things correspond "in some respect" (non-perfectly), then we would have to specify whether it were true that they corresponded in that "respect."

P 2.2: We cannot specify whether it were true that they corresponded in that respect [without first knowing what truth is].

C2: Therefore, two things can't correspond "in some respect" (non-perfectly).

Argument 3 (A3):

P 3.1: If we give a definition of truth as correspondence (or any definition of truth), then we have to specify the characteristic of correspondence.

P 3.2: We cannot specify characteristics of correspondence [because we would have to know if it were true beforehand that the characteristics were present].

C3: Therefore, we can't give a definition of truth as correspondence.

Arguments 1–3 lead Frege to claim the following: "Consequently it is probable that the content of the word 'true' is unique and indefinable" (p. 291). This is not quite deflationism, but it is an attempt to get rid of any robust metaphysics of correspondence. Let us examine the soundness of each argument in turn.

In A1, the second premise (1.2) seems uncontroversial. Correspondence theories, such as those considered in Chapters 6–8 are realistic. They maintain that the *adequation* in a correspondence relation is between thing and intellect, and that thing and intellect are fundamentally two different kinds of things.

The premise at issue then is 1.1. Must the relation of perfect correspondence entail identity? I think that the answer is yes. But, Frege seems to assume in this argument that it is impossible to have identity across difference. For example, consider a property such as being square. If one were to look at a floor covered with square tiles, one would see that the exact same property of being square or squareness is exemplified across different tiles.[1] If it is possible for the same universal or property to be present across different instances which exemplify the property, then it does not follow that if two different things correspond (in terms of exemplifying the same property), then they must be identical or must be *one* instead of *two* things.

The relation of correspondence is different than the multiple exemplification of a universal or property across different instances. The truth of premise 1.2 makes sure of that. The intellect or mind is not identical with reality. Thus, the way in which a universal (e.g., squareness) is related to a mind will be different than the way in which the same universal is related to the thing which exemplifies it. When I form a belief such as "the tile is rectangular."[2] I form a thought which does not exemplify rectangularity in the way the tile does, but nevertheless, my thought of the tile being rectangular is related to the universal/property of rectangularity. My thought exemplifies the property of being *about* rectangularity, and the tile on the floor exemplifies the property rectangularity. The identity between thought and object lies in the relation that both object and thought stand to the universal property of rectangularity.[3] Thus, premise 1.1 is false. Two things can correspond perfectly because of the presence of the same universal exemplified in them without being identical particular things.

In arguments 2 and 3, the key issues are premises 2.2 and 3.2, respectively. Whenever we attempt to specify a "respect" or "characteristics" of the correspondence relation, according to Frege, we are simply unable to do so. We are unable to do so because we first have to know what truth is. This generates a vicious circle or infinite regress. We can't say what the characteristics of truth are without knowing if it is *true* that a particular relation has those characteristics, and in order to know if it is *true* that a particular relation has those characteristics, we would have to know those particular characteristics.[4]

The simplest way to get out of this problem is to appeal to a direct awareness of the correspondence relation in simple acts of seeing things as they are thought to be. For example, Frege states, "If I do not know that a picture is meant to represent Cologne Cathedral then I do not know with what to compare the picture to decide on its truth" (Frege 1956, p. 291). Why not simply look at the picture? This gives you all the information that you need to find out if the thing the picture presents actually exists. You might not know that it is a "cathedral" or that it is in Cologne. But once you've seen the picture, you've got all you need to find that which corresponds to it.

Consider the belief that my keys are on my desk. Suppose that I use this belief to go and look at my desk. If the keys are there, then the belief is true, and I can experience that truth. If the keys are not there, the belief is false, and I can experience this as well. This is quite simple. In no part of the act of finding the world as it is believed to be need I specify a criterion of correspondence. In fact, the belief itself specifies what would be required for it to be true. The intentional properties of the belief which are about the world give us the requisite conditions for the belief to be true. Thus, contradictory to 2.2 and 3.2, we don't have to know that it is true that the criteria for correspondence are present before we see truth exemplified in acts of finding the world as it was thought to be. Thus, Frege's arguments to the conclusion that "the attempt to explain truth as correspondence collapses" (p. 291) are unsound.

Frege's next key move as a precursor to deflationism is his argument to the conclusion that the word "true" does not add anything to a sentence that is asserted. The two sentences, "p" and "it is true that p" have the same content, according to Frege. Let us look at the key aspect of this argument. Here is a direct quotation of the argument.

> It may nevertheless be thought that we cannot recognize a property of a thing without at the same time realizing the thought that this thing has this property to be true. So with every property of a thing is joined a property of a thought, namely, that of truth. It is also worthy of notice that the sentence: "I smell the scent of violets" has just the same content as the sentence "it is true that I smell the scent of violets." So it seems, then, that nothing is added to the thought by my ascribing to it the property of truth (p. 293).

Here is a simplification of Frege's argument:

> Argument 4 (A4)
> P 4.1: We can't recognize a property R of object O without realizing that my thought p "O has R" is true.
> P 4.2: "p" has same content as "it is true that p."
> C4: Nothing is added to the thought p by ascribing the property of truth to it.

Here is one reason to think that this conclusion does not follow. Consider two sentences:

> I. P
> II. P is true.

According to Frege, I and II have the same content. If two sentences have the same content, they should have the same logical implications; or rather the same logical inferences should be derivable from both; or rather the same knowledge should flow from both. However, the following example shows that this is false. Consider the following proposition, and assume that the truth value for Q is actually false.

> III. Q $\rightarrow$ P

Suppose we want to know if III is true or not by conducting a simple truth table. Assuming that Q is true, if I and II had the same content, we should be able to determine the truth of III from I, but we can't. I can't determine anything logically about III from an examination of I. It is only from the content of II that allows us to determine that III is true. Therefore, I and II don't have the same content. II implies that III would be true, but I does not. We cannot determine the truth value of a complex proposition without knowing the truth value of the simple proposition, but I does not tell us the truth value of the simple proposition. Thus, it cannot tell us the truth value of III. II does give us the truth value of III. If I and II had the same content, we should be able to determine the truth value of III from I, knowing that Q is true. I doesn't tell us the truth value of P, but II does, therefore they don't have the same content.

This type of counterexample to the claim that *p* and "it is true that *p*" shows that these two propositions do not have the same content. This is a starting point for a general critique of the deflationist project of eliminating truth as a substantive concept. If these propositions do not have the same content, then when "is true" is added to the proposition *p*, the locution "is true" is reflecting something more than what is present in the proposition itself as a mere assertion.

Let us turn to a fifth and final argument which Frege presents. Frege distinguishes between what he calls thinking (apprehending a thought), judging (recognizing the truth of a thought), and asserting (manifesting or communicating a judgment) (p. 294). Frege does think that we can communicate or "express" a thought without asserting that it is true (p. 294). He also maintains that when we recognize truth in a judgment, we "declare the recognition of truth in the form of an indicative sentence" (p. 294), but he claims that we don't need the word "true" in order to do this. When we make an assertion, the word "true" is irrelevant, and he concludes, "This explains why it is that nothing seems to be added to a thought by attributing to it the property of truth" (p. 295). But there seems to be a problem here.

These three claims seem to pull against each other.

i. We can "express the thought without laying it down as true."

ii. We declare the recognition of truth in the form of an indicative sentence

iii. "We do not have to use the word 'true' for this" (p. 294).

Frege's argument can be reconstructed as follows:

Argument 5 (A5)

5.1 If a thought is recognized as true, then the truth of the thought can be declared in an indicative sentence.

5.2 If the truth of the thought is declared in an indicative sentence, then we don't have to add the word true to the indicative sentence to communicate this.

5.3 We can recognize thoughts to be true.

C5 Therefore, we don't have to add the word "true" to the indicative sentence to communicate this.

My worry for this argument is 5.2. Do we need the word "true" to distinguish between linguistic expressions which refer to the phenomenal content of acts of thinking, judging, or asserting?

When Frege says that we can express a thought without "laying it down as true" I am assuming here that we can believe, think, say, or write some proposition *p*, without an assertion of whether *p* is true. This is what he calls "thinking" or merely apprehending a thought. Yet, when we write down or say what we are thinking, we do so by means of language often by means of physical inscriptions. This is where the trouble comes in.

Consider the sentence, "The cat is on the mat." As a sentence, this can be used to communicate a thought, judgment, or an assertion. I can use the same linguistic expression to communicate to another person that I am thinking, judging, or asserting.

Consider the following scenario. Suppose my cat has gone missing, and my wife asks me, "What are you thinking about the cat?" I say, "The cat is on the mat." A few minutes later, I open the back door to the house, and there the cat is, sitting on the mat. I look at the cat on the mat, and this experience matches my thought. Now I form a judgment, and I call out involuntarily, "The cat is on the mat." Suppose my wife yells back, "I heard you the first time, that's what you are thinking about the cat, but we still don't know where she is." Now, I yell back a third time, "The cat is on the mat." Now, I really want to communicate to her, not only my thought, and the reality of my judgment, but also the assertion that the cat is on the mat. Finally, a bit exasperated, my wife yells back down, "I heard you the first two times … quit yelling and go find the stupid cat."

In this example, the exact same utterance (assuming it has the same tone or timbre in the expression), or the same inscription (suppose we were texting each other) could be used three times with no distinction between whether I was using the sentence to communicate a thought, judgment or assertion. In Frege's sense, each exemplification of the sentence "The cat is on the mat" contains the same "thought." But the word "true" helps us to distinguish the type of exemplification of the sentence (act of thinking, judging or asserting). The word "true" gives us a way of distinguishing between these three. When used in an indicative sentence it refers to the real experience had in an act of what Frege calls judging. Put another way, it refers to the act of seeing the match between the thought and the world. The assertion is the communication of the awareness of this act of seeing the way things are, or it could be used to express the potentiality of such act. Thus, the word "true," contrary to what Frege argues, does add something to the mere use of a sentence. This implies that "P is true" cannot be deflated to "P."

The acts of thinking, judging, and asserting which Frege distinguishes seem right. Considered from a first person perspective, considered phenomenologically, the "what it is like to experience" an act of thinking, judging, and asserting varies widely. The word "true" applies primarily to judgment: the direct experience of finding the world as it was thought to be, to the "belief that p is true." It is from these simple acts of finding the world to be as we thought it to be that we derive our concept of truth and use the word "true" to apply to those specific acts. The word "true" could not be used as a predicate for a sentence which refers to an act of thinking. Thought just is the presentation of concepts before the mind. In acts of mere thinking there is no awareness of a matching of thought to reality; thus, the word "true" should not be applied to such acts. Even according to Frege, acts of asserting are derived from acts of judging. Thus, if the word "true" applies primarily to acts of judging, then it should only be applied to acts of asserting derivatively from acts of judging.[5] Thus, any attempt to use Frege's ideas in "The Thought" to justify a version of deflationism about truth will fail.

5.2 Horwich

Paul Horwich is one of the more recent advocates of a deflationist view of truth. From the very beginning of his book *Truth* he claims the following: "The common-sense notion that truth is a kind of 'correspondence with facts' has never been worked out to anyone's satisfaction. Even its advocates would concede that it remains little more than a vague, guiding intuition" (Horwich 1990, p. 1). The book you are now reading does *not* concede that the reality of correspondence is "little more than a vague guiding intuition" (see especially Chapters 7 and 8). In fact, I affirm that correspondence is a reality with which everyone is familiar. Correspondence is a robust concept which is precisely how truth should be understood. It is such a clear and helpful concept that other versions of truth fall far short in their ability to capture our experience of truth. Deflationism is one such view of truth. In this section, I try to give a few reasons why I think that the very notion of deflationism is mistaken.

Horwich claims that his ideas are not new. He maintains that he is following similar lines of thinking about truth found in Frege, Wittgenstein, Ramsey, Ayer, Strawson, and Quine. Horwich sets out to defend the idea that truth as it has been considered in the history of philosophy is trivial and mundane.[6] It is simple and not particularly mysterious or deep. This deflationist theory of truth expresses a stark minimalism where the concept of truth is best expressed simply by the biconditional "equivalence schema":

It is true *that p* if and only if p

It is important to note that this is all truth is. Truth is nothing more than the "truth predicate" that is, the locution "is true." According to Horwich, this predicate "exists solely for the sake of a certain logical need" (p. 2). When we want to express belief (or some other attitude toward a proposition) but we are ignorant of what the proposition is, the truth predicate ("is true") "enables the construction of another proposition … which is perfectly appropriate as the alternative object of our attitude" (p. 3). In other words, the truth predicate ("is true") is merely a linguistic device. Truth itself is deflated to a function of language. Let us look at Horwich's argument to this conclusion. His argument goes like this:

P1. What Oscar said is true.
P2. P1 is of the form "x is F."
P3. Assume: x = the proposition p
P4. Therefore, we can infer *p* (p. 3).

One way to think of this argument is that by substituting the subject of P1 "What Oscar said" with "the proposition *p*" it is possible to derive or infer *p*. So from the proposition "*p* is true" it follows that "*p*."

There are at least two problems with this initial deflationist argument. First, it is not at all clear from the claim "The proposition p is true" that "p" follows at all in any way that is non-trivial. In a trivial way it is correct to say that "p" follows from "the proposition p is true." The general form of "the proposition p is true" is simply an "x is F" statement. F here is the truth predicate "is true." In a trivial way, of course "p" does follow from "the proposition p is true." One could mean by "follows" that "we can infer it to exist." This is trivial because, we can infer that the subject of any statement exists (or is asserted to exist) when a predicate is attached to that subject. From the existence of the predicate we can infer that the subject exists. So, trivially then, "p" follows from the statement "the proposition p is true."

Second, it is not clear that the formality of this argument allows for "p" to be inferred from (or even follows logically from) "the proposition p is true." In Horwich's P3 above, he allows for the idea that by logical substitution the subject clause "the proposition p" can logically replace x in premise P2's "x is F." The problem stems from the common translation techniques that are introduced in introductory logic textbooks (see Hurley 2012). Standard translation techniques for a generalization or universal statement such as "The proposition p is true" (as opposed to a singular or particular statement) would be translated into general universal quantification notation as: (x) (Px → Tx). In plain English, this would read, "For all x, if x is a proposition, then x is true". This would serve as the first premise in an argument looking like this:

P1': $(x) (Px \rightarrow Tx)$ [The proposition p is true]. Premise

P2': Pp [*p* is the proposition P]. Premise

P3': $Pp \rightarrow Tp$ Universal instantiation from P1'

C': Tp P2', P3' *modus ponens*

But translating back into English from formal logical notation, the conclusion of the argument is, C' isn't *p*. C' is "*p* is true." "*p* is true" is distinct from *p*. In other words, there seems to be some logical sleight of hand going on here, where Horwich simply jettisons the predicate from the subject without strictly speaking following what is allowed by the simple inference.

There seems to be some equivocation on how a predicate is applied in this argument. For in the substitution instance in P2′, Horwich wants to be able to claim that "Whatever Oscar said is true" which has a truth predicate to function as any *x is F*. But, he says earlier "Unlike most other predicates, 'is true should not be expected to participate in some deep theory of that to which it refers…Thus its assimilation to superficially similar expressions is misleading" (p. 2). Yet, in the substitution instance the truth predicate is supposed to fit nicely into an *x is F* type of statement. It doesn't seem to be able to be both ways. Thus, Horwich's initial argument for deflationism either gives us a conclusion which is trivial (from the fact that a proposition is true, that proposition exists), or is simply a non-sequitur. Either way, the deflationist point hasn't been established.

Horwich maintains that "Truth is captured by the schema, ⟨p⟩ is true ↔ p" (p. 263). The equivalence scheme basically says that all propositions are true if and only if the proposition is maintained or asserted or stated, where asserting a proposition entails asserting it to be true. This is no different than Frege's claim above in Section 5.1. According to Horwich, accounts of truth which try to go beyond the deflationary equivalence scheme and say that a proposition is made true by a fact or state of affairs, or reality or something else will always fall prey to the objection that one will have to be committed to funny sorts of facts. For example, the proposition "*p* or *q*" would be made true by a fact which is disjunctive, or a bit of reality which is disjunctive. A proposition like "If *p* then *q*" would have to be made true by a counterfactual fact or a bit of counterfactual reality. This would require an ontology of facts or reality which would be rather exotic, and this supposedly counts as a good reason to reject "truth making" views of truth.

Truthmaking, according to Horwich, is really just *explaining* why something is true. To say that a proposition is made true by reality is to explain that it is true because reality is the way it is (p. 265). He goes on to argue that since truthmaking is really just a way of explaining why something is true, that it is not even possible for a fact (or any other truth maker) to *make* a proposition true (p. 265). He offers three arguments which entail that "it is *never* possible for the fact that p to make true the proposition that p" (p. 265). We will look at each of these in turn.

Horwich claims that when we explain why a proposition like "<Mars is red> is true, we first deduce Mars is red from some combination of laws of physics and initial conditions" (p. 265). Second, we use the equivalence schema "⟨Mars is red⟩ is true ↔ Mars is red...to deduce why ⟨Mars is red⟩ is true, which *explains* why ⟨Mars is red⟩ is true. Third, this entails ⟨Mars is red⟩ is true because Mars is red which can be generalized to ⟨p⟩ is true because p" (p. 266). This is of course the deflationist's point. Truth is nothing more than the equivalence scheme: It is true *that p* if and only if p. Therefore, "It is *never* possible for the fact that p to make true the proposition that p." (p. 265).

Here is a more formalized version of this argument (A1) with the premises listed out with their corresponding justification.

1.1	p	Deduced from evidence
1.2	⟨p⟩ is true ↔ p	Invoked to explain why p is true
1.3:.	p → ⟨p⟩	From 1.1, 1.2 equivalence and *modus ponens*.

The same will go for facts, according to Horwich.

1.1 *p	Deduced from evidence
1.2 *The fact that p exists ↔ p	Invoked for the purpose of explanation
1.3 *Therefore, p → the fact that p exists	From 1.1, 1.2 equivalence and *modus ponens*.

Thus, according to Horwich, it is *because* p that ⟨p⟩ is true, and it is *because* p that the fact that p exists. But, this is exactly the other way around from what the truth making approach maintains. That view maintained that the proposition was made true by the fact, but what Horwich seeks to demonstrates is that that the assertion of the proposition *p* is what entails the fact that *p* exists. The assertion of the proposition is what entails that the proposition is true.

There are several worries with these valid arguments. My first concern is with the first premise of each argument. Horwich says that we deduce p from evidence. But, what exactly is deduction? It is a type of logical inference by means of which the mind sees the way things are through or by means of the evidence present in the logical relations. More precisely, a deductive argument is a set of propositions in which the premises claim that if they are true, it is impossible for the conclusion to be false.

The justification for premise 1.1 and 1.1* is that it is deduced. In one sense, deducing p is simply seeing that p follows logically from other evidence. We see this in rationally perceiving the validity of a deduction in an instance of *modus ponens*:

1. *s*
2. *s→ p*
3:. *p.*

We can deduce *p* from 1 and 2. Understanding *modus ponens* (or perhaps an AAA figure 1) is a way of seeing that *p* is true, only if 1 and 2 are true. In other words, the concept of truth is already presupposed in the act of deducing (or inducing). Seeing that the argument is valid is a way of seeing its truth. You see *p* because you see that the deduction from which *p* is the conclusion is deductively valid (it is impossible that if the premises are true that the conclusion could be false).

However, there is more to a deduction than validity. Deductions are also sound or unsound. A deduction is sound only if it is valid *and* has all true premises. When Horwich says that we deduce *p*, he is presupposing some notion of truth which makes the premises of the deduction true and entails the *soundness* of the deduction. If we deduce one side of the equivalence schema *p*, we are deducing it from a sound argument, which means that all the premises of the argument are true. Thus, Horwich is using a notion of deduction which requires an antecedent account of truth to explain the difference between a sound and an unsound deduction in order to establish one side of the biconditional in his equivalence schema which is supposed to *be* the account of truth. The right hand side of the biconditional, which is supposed to tell us what truth is, cannot be established without first telling us what a sound argument is. That cannot be done by using the equivalence schema.

The second worry is with the equivalence scheme itself: ⟨p⟩ is true ↔ p. When considering this scheme, there is a dilemma which is faced due to the presence of the biconditional operator. On a common understanding of the logical propositional operators, biconditionals are true only when both sides of the logical operator are true or when both sides are false. If the left hand side and the right hand side of the biconditional really assert the same thing, then they literally are the same proposition which would give us $P ↔ P$. This makes the equivalence scheme a tautology. It is necessarily true. This is somewhat philosophically interesting, as a necessary truth, but one will still want to know what it means for P to be true.

Think of it this way. If the equivalence scheme is nothing more than $P ↔ P$ is that it is derivable from P. Thus, $P ↔ P$ is simply another way of saying that P is either true or false. This is to say that the equivalence scheme tells us nothing more than for any proposition p, p is either true or false. This is correct. Propositions are true or false. Saying this does not tell us what truth amounts to.

If the equivalence scheme is not reducible to the tautology $P ↔ P$, then that means that the right hand side of the conditional and the left hand side are not the same proposition. If they are not the same proposition, then the equivalence scheme is contingent, and once again the biconditional will be true when both sides are true or both sides are false. This means that the biconditional must be derived by the conjunction of two conditionals: ⟨p⟩ is true → p and p → ⟨p⟩ is true. The question becomes, how does one establish the truth of either of these conditionals? One establishes it by establishing the truth of both sides. If the biconditional is true, then one side can't be true and the other false. So, we need to check to see if one side is true. One side of each conditional is a proposition. How do we establish whether one side is true? To do that we would need to know what it means for one side to be true.

So, we now ask, what is it for p to be true or what makes p true, or what does it mean to say that p is true? It seems circular to say that p is true if and only if p, since this is exactly what we are trying to find out. The equivalence scheme itself cannot establish its own truth without specifying apart from itself what it means for it to be true. For example, how does one explain what it is for the right hand side of the following instance of the equivalence scheme to be true:

> ES1: It is true that <the cat is on the mat> if and only if, the cat is on the mat.
>
> ES1 is a conjunction of
>
> ES1.1 If it is true that <the cat is on the mat>, then the cat is on the mat
>
> and
>
> ES1.2 If the cat is on the mat, then it is true that <the cat is on the mat>.

The problem is especially problematic for ES1.2. Suppose I want to know what it means for the antecedent of the conditional in ES1.2 to be true. The deflationist response would be "the cat is on the mat" is true if and only if the cat is on the mat. However, the equivalence scheme, ES1 is what I am trying to establish as true. If I try to explain what it is for the antecedent of ES1.2 to be true by means of the equivalence scheme ES1, then I am using ES1 to show how the right hand side of the conditional ES1.2 is true. This is circular. One can't explain what is for the biconditional to be true by appealing to the biconditional itself.

Thus, we have seen that the use of the equivalence scheme is either trivial or circular. It asserts nothing more than any proposition is either true or false, or it attempts to tell us what its own truth value is by means of itself. Neither of these prospects is particularly promising.

5.3 Conclusion

Deflationism as we have considered it here is enticing. It attempts to make simple what can become very complex. There is something right about deflationism, in that it attempts to display the simplicity of truth. However, it does not make sense of our ordinary experiences of finding the world as we believed it to be. These types of experiences are the common core of what we know about truth. If deflationism as expressed in the equivalence scheme were correct, it would not rule out, at least according to Horwich, the real ways in which a proposition is true because of the way the world is. Horwich maintains, "It is indeed undeniable that whenever a proposition or an utterance is true, it is true *because* something in the world is a certain way" (Horwich 2000, p. 105). This idea *is* consistent with our common experience of finding the world as it was thought to be, but this (as we saw above) functions in a mere explanatory sense for the deflationist. It does not tell us about what truth is in our ordinary experiences, and this is what a theory of truth ought to do.

6

Correspondence

6.0 Introduction

I reach for my keys in my backpack to unlock my car. They are not there. I believe that I have left my keys on my desk. I return to my office (the secretary lets me in for the third time this semester), and I look on my desk. I see my keys. I swipe them off the desk, mumble my apologies again to the secretary, call my wife to let her know I'll be late (again), and head to my car.

When I see that my keys are on my desk where I had believed them to be, I see the correspondence of my belief with reality. This is a common event. What is not as common as the event itself is a thorough analysis of the constituent parts of the event. Such an analysis of our beliefs matching reality is called a correspondence theory of truth.

In this chapter, I begin with a brief lexical definition of "correspondence" to give us a feel for what this concept could mean. Then I sketch briefly some possible relata in the correspondence relation, pointing out the strengths and weaknesses of each possible combination. Finally, I give an overview of three correspondence theories in the last century or so.[1] I will examine Bertrand Russell and Ludwig Wittgenstein's analytic approaches, and John Austin's semantic approach as recently presented by Gerald Vision. I argue that each account fails to take into account the metaphysics that are required in order for a mental state (such as a belief) to correspond adequately to things outside the mind. In the next chapter, I will present a survey of Edmund Husserl's phenomenological view of correspondence which I believe fills this ontological gap in the theories considered in this chapter.

6.1 Lexical description of "correspondence"

What is meant when a philosopher talks of truth as "correspondence"? Here are a few lexical aids with which we can begin to understand the notion of correspondence as it is used in the English language. The prefix "co" usually means something like "with" or "together" or similarity of degree. The prefix "re" often means "again" or "anew." The Latin verb "spondere" is associated with a promise to return or "answer" (*correspondence* 1990). By definition the word "correspondence" implies that there are at least two things which stand in some sort of relation with each other. This peculiar relation is one in which the related things are "together again" or "together repeatedly," and they "*spondere*," "make an answer," or "react" one to another. But the word "correspondence" does not tell us anything about the nature of the things which are so related. If one desires an account of truth, and wants to use the word "correspondence" to say something interesting about what truth is, then one must say something about both the items which enter into this relation and the relation itself.

6.2 The possible relata of the correspondence relation

What are the things involved in the relation of correspondence as it is used to describe truth? Here are a few candidates:

> minds (thoughts/beliefs/concepts within minds)
>
> things (any object whatsoever)
>
> propositions (abstract entities existing independently of minds which can be of any object)[2]
>
> facts (mind independent entities which are of and generated by existing things)

There are at least twelve possible relations among these items:

1 mind/mind

2 mind/proposition

3 mind/thing

4 mind/thing/proposition

5 mind/thing/fact

6 mind/thing/proposition/fact

7 thing/proposition

8 thing/fact

9 thing/proposition/fact

10 mind/fact

11 mind/proposition/fact

12 proposition/fact

Before various difficulties with these relations are addressed, a word must be said about the selection of these items. It is important to note that item 1 on this list is the only item where one of the four candidates is repeated. The other candidates are not listed twice, because if they were, the result would be either (a) a relation between entirely different things, propositions, or facts, or (b) a relation between the same proposition, thing, or fact. Result (a) is unacceptable. If "correspondence" is to make sense at all, there must be some way in which the two things, propositions, or facts are similar to one another. However, if they are entirely different, then correspondence which involves some relation of similarity cannot occur. Result (b) is also unacceptable. If the two things, propositions, or facts are identical, then the relation of correspondence collapses into the relation of identity. Therefore, in the twelve options above, neither things, propositions, nor facts are repeated.

However, there are at least two reasons that the relation of mind/mind is acceptable in ways that thing/thing, proposition/proposition, or fact/fact are not. First, with minds (thoughts, beliefs, or concepts within minds) there is the possibility of two different minds entertaining the same thought, belief, or concept. Thus, truth might consist in the relation of two minds entertaining the same thought, belief, or concept. Second, one individual mind can entertain similar thoughts, beliefs, or concepts. One's mind can at the same time entertain similar thoughts of what the world is like where the coherence of the relations between one's thoughts, beliefs, or concepts putatively determines what is true about the world.

Several of these candidates for the related items in the correspondence relation have obvious difficulties. As indicated above, there are two ways to understand the first candidate for what the relata of the correspondence relation are (mind/mind). The first way to understand this candidate, is of two minds related in such a way that the thoughts/beliefs/concepts of the first mind "correspond" to the thoughts/beliefs/concepts of the second (or more) mind(s). If this candidate were understood in this way, a problem immediately arises. If truth as correspondence consists of relations between minds alone, then the independence of truth would be sacrificed.

It is possible for a proponent of a correspondence theory of truth to hold truth to be something that is independent of what an individual or groups of individuals think. One proposition which is putatively independent of all human minds is the proposition that there were rocks before there were people.[3] This proposition is and was true before there were human minds to think about their being rocks before people. Another example illustrates the nature of the independence of truth from belief. Suppose Smith's belief that *p* corresponds with Jones' belief that *p*, where *p* is "there is gas in the tank of the car in which Smith and Jones are now traveling." The correspondence of Smith's belief that *p* to Jones' belief that *p* will not help them reach their destination if in fact their gas tank is empty, regardless of how much their beliefs correspond or how tenaciously they believe *p*.

The second way to understand the first candidate for the relata of the correspondence relation mind/mind is that truth consists in the correspondence of similar thoughts/beliefs/concepts within one individual mind. If this is how truth as correspondence is understood, then one is faced with the difficulty of showing how mere coherence of similar beliefs within minds can make those beliefs true.

A final difficulty which applies to either understanding of mind/mind is the difficulty of relativism that either leads to an infinite regress of correspondence relations or is self-defeating. Relation 1, mind/mind, makes truth relative to the correspondence of beliefs between several minds or within an individual's mind. If some individual (or group of individuals) S maintains that truth is correspondence of beliefs within S's mind (or between several minds), then S is committed to the truth of the relativistic proposition (RP): truth is the correspondence of beliefs within S's mind (or between the minds of the group). This proposition is true because either (i) it corresponds with other beliefs within S's mind (or between the minds of the group), or (ii) because it corresponds with something other than beliefs (some other sense of correspondence in 2–12 above) within S's mind (or between the minds of the group). If S maintains that RP is true because of (i), then S is committed to a further proposition RP': RP is true because it corresponds with other beliefs within S's mind (or between the minds of the group). This leads to an infinite regress of correspondence relations within S's mind (or between the minds of the group). If S maintains that PR is true because of (ii), then S's claim is self-defeating, PR itself is not true based on correspondence with S's other beliefs. Any positive claim that relation 1 as a claim about truth being relative to correspondence of thoughts/beliefs/concepts within S's mind (or between the minds of a group) either leads to an infinite regress of correspondence relations or is self-defeating. Thus, the relata in relation 1 ought to be rejected as the relata of the correspondence view of truth.

Relation 2 has the difficulty of making truth unrelated to the world.[4] Correspondence between proposition and mind alone is too broad. If the correspondence relation is understood to be a relation between propositions and minds, then many absurdities will arise. First, assume that propositions *qua* abstract entities which can be of any logically possible object exist independently of human minds. From this assumption, it follows that the proposition (p): "the moon is made of green cheese" exists as an abstract entity. Second, assume that some mind S is now, was, or will be thinking/believing/conceiving (p') the moon is made of green cheese. From these assumptions, if truth is understood as correspondence between (p) and (p'), then it is true that the moon is made of green cheese just in case (p) corresponds to (p'). But, is it true that the moon is made of green cheese? Surely it is not. More is needed to understand the nature of truth than merely the correspondence between propositions and thoughts.

Relation 3 is essentially St. Thomas Aquinas' understanding of truth involving things and the intellect. Aquinas maintained that "'true' expresses the correspondence of being with the knowing power [of the mind] for all knowing is produced by an assimilation of the knower to the thing known so that assimilation is said to be the cause of knowledge" (Aquinas 1952, Question 1: Article 1). This is the notion of truth as the "adequation of thing and intellect."

There are at least two potential difficulties with this relation, which equally applies to relations 4–9. First, in these cases, "things" are one of the related items. However, things can quit existing, and if a thing quits existing, do we want to say that there is no longer anything truth?[5] This might be solvable by an adequate account of time. On one view of time, anything which exists, whether it exists past present or future actually exists simultaneously at all times. This is usually called a "B" series or tenseless view of time. On another view of time, a tensed or "A" series view of time, things either did exist, now exist, or will exist.

So either on a tensed or tenseless view of time, there can be truths about things even though they do not exist at present. But, assuming that a tensed view of time is more reasonable to believe than a tenseless view of time (e.g., that dinosaurs no longer exist, that the past does not now exist, but the past existed, and the future will exist) there is a problem with any relation where the corresponding relata quit existing. If one of the relata ceases to exist, then the relation itself ceases to exist. Relation 3 limits truth to times where things exist. Unless there are other entities which are (a) independent of the things themselves, (b) are about the things themselves (contain in some sense the properties of the things themselves at all times), and (c) can serve as the "truth makers" of those things with which the mind can be adequated, then it may be wise to rule out any view of truth as correspondence that requires the continued existence of things.

One might, however, maintain that truth as a relationship between mind and thing, where a thing may no longer exist, but the thing qua past existent and its correspondence to a mind might fit the bill. This might require an account of facts where facts are the "ontic residue" of things which once existed. So, for example, it is true that George Washington was the first president of the United States, just in case there is a mind which is adequated to the thing of George Washington's being the first president of the United States. If there is now no such thing as George Washington's being the first president of the United States, then how can my mind be adequated with that thing? One could say that either the mind is adequated with something that was the case, or one could say that the mind is now adequated with the fact that George Washington is the first president of the United States. Either way, it still seems plausible that relation 3, the relation of correspondence between mind and thing, is reasonable.

A second difficulty with relation 3 as well as relations 4, 5, 6, 10, and 11 is that they each have minds as one of the related items. However, if there were no minds, would there still be truth? Without minds, relation 3 would be reduced to mere things, and there would no longer be any correspondence at all. Relation 4 would be reduced to 7, 5 to 8, 6 to 9, 10 to facts (again there is no longer a correspondence relation) and 11 to 12. Although Aquinas' understanding of truth requires minds (at least a Divine mind), certain propositions could *possibly* be true even though there were no human minds. Is it the case that before there were human minds, the proposition "there are x number of craters on the moon" was true? The requirement of human minds for the possibility of truth may seem too strong. There are propositions which are possibly true regardless of any human mind thinking of those propositions. Without minds, truth would be a potentiality in the cosmos, but not an actuality.

The remaining options are 7, 8, 9 and 12 involving three entities: things, propositions, and facts. The most complex relation, the relation that involves all three entities is 11: the relation between thing/proposition/fact. What are the existential dependencies among these items? Can a thing exist without a proposition? This depends on what one takes propositions to be. Is does not seem impossible that there can be propositions without human minds. Although it doesn't seem implausible that there can be no propositions without human minds; there certainly can be no sentences or statements. Assuming that there can be propositions without human minds, might truth be a relation between things and propositions? Yes, but again there is the problem of things ceasing to exist. There are still truths about things which no longer exist.

To sum up, relation 1 has the difficulties of sacrificing the independence of truth, of the unintelligibility of being able to produce truth from mere coherence, and of the infinite regress and self-defeating nature generated by relativism. 2 has the weakness of being too broad. 3 through 6, 10, and 11 depend on human minds, which imply that truth is possible, but not actual before there were human minds. 3 through 9 depend on things, but there are truths about things which no longer exist. This leaves relation 12 where facts might be understood as entities which result from things being true, whether or not those things now exist.[6] Relation 12 is not free of difficulties. The existence of propositions and facts must be defended in such a way that the properties of these entities are such that they can be related in a way that makes sense of the general notions of correspondence. In addition, without minds, truth will be a mere possibility.

When we analyze the phenomena of coming to find the world as we thought it to be, the act of experiencing truth, we have an awareness of both mind (ours) and the thing itself. Facts may be involved and propositions may be involved, but the most basic relationship is between thing and intellect. Any further development of the correspondence relation should be focused here. We will return to this in Husserl's view of truth in Chapter 7.

This has been a brief sketch about the possible relations of correspondence. It is important to remember that by definition correspondence involves some kind of similarity, equivalence, or matching. Most accounts of correspondence will try to make sense of both what the items are that are related in the relation, and the manner in which they are related. Understanding truth as correspondence involves two things. First, it involves understanding some general sense of what the relation amounts to (i.e., similarity, equivalence, or matching). Second, it involves a description of the properties of the related entities which adequately express how the general notion of correspondence obtains. We turn now to a few of the major correspondence approaches over the last century.

6.3 Bertrand Russell

Bertrand Russell considers the question of truth to be one of the fundamental questions in philosophy (Russell 1910, p. 115). His views on truth are discussed throughout his philosophical works. Russell was committed to a correspondence view of truth, but he had several different versions of a correspondence theory over his long career. First, Russell changed his mind as to the exact nature of the subject that enters into the correspondence relation. In his *My Philosophical Development* (1959), Russell claims that his view of truth had changed because of his change in his view of the subject. He indicates that he changed his mind between the view expressed in *Philosophical Essays* (1910) and his "On Propositions: what they are and how they mean" (1919) due to the influence of William James. In this 1919 paper, Russell gives the reason why he rejects the "subject," that is, under the influence of William James.

He states that the act or subject is,

schematically convenient, but not empirically discoverable. It seems to serve the same sort of purpose as is served by points and instants...All these things have to be *constructed*, not postulated: they are not the stuff of the world, but assemblages which it is convenient to be able to designate as if they were single things.

(Russell 1919, pp. 305–306)

Russell reiterates his view of his rejection of the subject in his 1959 work *My Philosophical Development*. He states,

> My own definition of "truth," at that earlier time, was published in the last chapter of *Philosophical Essays* [Russell 1910]. I had, later, to abandon this theory because it depended upon the view that sensation is an essentially relational occurrence [between an object and a subject]—a view which, as explained in an earlier chapter, I abandoned under the influence of William James ... I had to find a new theory to allow for the rejection of the "subject."
>
> (Russell 1959, pp. 181–182)

Thus, Russell's view of truth changed over the course of his life due to his decision to reject the existence of the subject as a part of the correspondence relation.

The second way that Russell's view of truth as correspondence changed is indicated in the 1959 quotation above where he states, "I no longer thought that a relation can occur significantly as a term, except when a paraphrase is possible in which it does not so occur" (1959, p. 182). His earlier views of truth (Russell 1910, 1912) rely on an understanding of how relations between objects enter into an act of judgment. For example, consider the two-term relation "A loves B." This two-term relation, if it exists, is a complex object composed of the following: A related to B by a relation of love. This complex object has a "sense" namely of "A loves B." If there is a judgment made by a subject (S), "that A loves B" this judgment is essentially a relation between S to A, and love, and B. This judgment also has a sense of "A loves B." The judgment is true when the complex object, with the same sense as the judgment, exists and is false otherwise. The subject, on this early view of truth is an intimate part of the judgment which is of the complex object. However, Russell comes to reject the notion that a relation, in this case the relation of loving between A and B, functions significantly as a term. What this rejection amounts to will be considered below. Suffice it for now to say that this is one of the significant changes that Russell made in his view of truth during his life.

Russell also changes his mind about what he takes the truth bearers of the correspondence relation to be. He gives a broad stroke account of truth bearers in 1910 indicating that statements, beliefs, or judgments are truth bearers (Russell 1910, p. 148). In 1919, he states that "propositions are the essential thing" (Russell 1919, p. 148). In 1927, he says that statements and by extension beliefs are truth bearers and reiterates that truth applies "primarily to a form of word and derivatively to a belief" (Russell 1927, pp. 254, 262). Then in 1940, he seems to change his mind and writes that truth and falsehood are "predicates, primarily of beliefs, and derivatively of sentences" (Russell 1940, p 227). He restates this view again in 1948 and 1959 that beliefs are primary and sentence secondary (Russell 1948, p. 112, Russell 1959, p. 183).

The shifts that occur are quite clear. In 1912, he speaks broadly of statements, beliefs, or judgments as the primary bearers of truth. In 1918, the proposition is the primary truth bearer "for formal purposes." Then, in 1927 Russell apparently changes his mind. In this work, he states that truth is prima facie applied to statements (forms of words) and derivatively or by extension to beliefs. Then in 1940, Russell seems to contradict himself, and revert back to the position that he was holding in 1918. He says here that truth is a predicate "primarily of beliefs, and derivatively of sentences." He repeats this position in 1948 and 1959 maintaining that beliefs are that to which truth belongs primarily and propositions and sentences only derivatively.

In three respects Russell changes his views about the elements of a correspondence view of truth: the nature of the subject, the nature of relations, and the nature of truth bearers. For these reasons, it is difficult to say that there is a Russellian view of truth as correspondence. There seem to be several. I will offer a critique of a revised Russellian view in section 6.5.

6.4 Ludwig Wittgenstein

In his *Tractatus Logico-Philosophicus*, Wittgenstein presents an account of truth as correspondence which is derived from an analysis of the nature of facts (truth makers), pictures, thoughts, and propositions (all of which function as truth bearers). His procedure in this work is as follows. First, he talks about the nature of the world and its divisibility into facts. Second, he discusses how facts are related to human minds through "pictures." Third, he presents his version of the correspondence view of truth which is an account of the connection between pictures, facts, thoughts and propositions. Fourth, he considers the use of the account of truth as correspondence in the development of propositional forms and logic. Fifth, he applies this account of truth as correspondence to logical structures. Sixth, he applies the generalizations of truth functions to logic and all propositions. Lastly, he concludes with silence about matters about which he is unable to speak. My focus will be on the first three of Wittgenstein's tasks in the *Tractatus*.

Wittgenstein's first task in the *Tractatus* is to give an account of the "truth maker" side of the correspondence relation. He understood truth makers to be facts, that is, components or divided parts of the world which are composed of combinations of simple objects in Sections 1.1 and 1.2 of the *Tractatus* (Wittgenstein 1961).[7] After laying out what he believes to be the nature of the world and facts, he proceeds to discuss what he believes to be the "truth bearer" side of the correspondence relation followed by the nature of the correspondence relation itself.

Wittgenstein's second task in the *Tractatus* is to explain his view of truth bearers through an account of "pictures." Wittgenstein describes pictures in terms of what they do. A picture "**presents** a situation in logical space, the existence and non-existence of states of affairs" (2.11), and **models** reality (2.12). Pictures "**have the elements of the picture corresponding** to them" (2.13), and those elements "are the **representatives** of objects" (2.131) (emphasis added). Although Wittgenstein claims that we "picture facts to ourselves" (2.1), he claims that "A picture is a fact" (2.141). What he means by this is that "every picture is a fact" qua one of the things into which the world divides. He does not mean that "every picture is a fact, *and* every fact is a picture," since he claims that the world qua totality of facts "is all that is the case" (1).

It is through pictures that facts are related to human minds. He states, "we picture facts to ourselves," and "the fact that the elements of a picture are related to one another in a determinate way represents that things are related to one another in the same way" (2.15).

How does this representation of a picture take place? Wittgenstein implies that a picture qua fact has a certain determinate structure or what he calls "pictorial form" which is the possibility of the structure of the connexion of the picture's elements (2.15). He states, "Pictorial form [the possibility of the structure of the connection of its elements] is the possibility that things are related to one another in the same way as the elements of the picture" (2.151). It is through a picture's "pictorial form," its possibility of "corresponding" with facts that generates truth as correspondence. It is through this possibility that there is a connection between picture and fact. Wittgenstein states, "*That* is how a picture is attached to reality; it reaches right out to it" (2.1511); "It is laid against reality like a measure" (2.1512). However, a "reaching right out to it" does not make an "attachment" any more than someone reaching out their hand to save a drowning man means that they have reached him. Wittgenstein must provide something to fill the ontological gap between picture and reality.

Wittgenstein proceeds to fill the gap between picture and reality by indicating that a picture has some correlation with facts. He states, "A picture ... includes the pictorial relationship [which] consists of the correlations of the picture's elements with things [facts]" (2.1513, 2.1514). He adds, "These correlations are ... the feelers of the picture's elements, with which the picture touches reality" (2.1515). The use of the term "correlation" is auspicious as it implies an identity between picture and fact which it touches. The identity is made even stronger when he states, "If a fact is to be a picture, it [a picture] must have something in common with what it [a picture] depicts [a fact]" (2.16).

This notion of "something in common" implies that there must be something that is *present in* both the fact and the picture which allow them to be correlated. Wittgenstein states, "There must be something identical in a picture and what it depicts, to enable the one to be a picture of the other at all" (2.161). The something identical, what picture and fact (reality) have in common is "pictorial form" (2.17). He elaborates, "What any picture, of whatever form, must have in common with reality, in order to be able to depict it—correctly or incorrectly—in any way at all, is logical form, i.e., the form of reality" (2.18). More explicitly he states, "A picture has logico-pictorial form in common with what it depicts" (2.2).

What exactly is pictorial form? A lengthy quotation is helpful in answering this question:

> 2.15 The fact that the elements of a picture are related to one another in a determinate way represents that things are related to one another in the same way.
>
> Let us call this connexion of its elements the structure of the picture, and let us call the possibility of this structure the pictorial form of the picture.
>
> 2.151 Pictorial form is the possibility that things are related to one another in the same way as the elements of the picture.

The "commonality," the "something identical" the "correlation" between picture and thought is simply the "possibility" of things being related to one another in a fact (states of affairs). This is analogous to the way the elements of the picture are related to one another. Thus, a picture represents "a *possibility* of existence and non-existence of states of affairs" (2.201), "a *possible* situation in logical space" (2.202), and "contains the *possibility* of the situation that it represents" (2.203). Wittgenstein says that the commonality, the identity, and the correlation between picture and fact (state of affairs) are a possibility of identical form.

What exactly does he mean by form? He indicates that "form" is the arrangement of the parts of a fact or state of affairs. He states, "The determinate way in which objects are connected in a state of affairs is the structure of the state of affairs" (2.032), and "form is the possibility of structure" (2.033). The structure of states of affairs is composed of a determinate interconnection of ultimately simple objects. The possibility of a structure in a state of affairs is the form of the state of affairs. When the form of a state of affairs is identical to the possibility represented by a picture, then the correspondence relation obtains.

The logical form of reality when it is identical to the pictorial form of a picture (which is itself a representation of a possible state of affairs), yields truth as correspondence. The words indicating Wittgenstein's emphasis on truth as correspondence is emphasized in the following quotations. He states,

2.21 A picture **agrees with** reality or **fails to agree**; it is correct or incorrect, true or false.

2.22 What a picture **represents** it represents independently of its truth or falsity, by means of its pictorial form . . . what a picture represents is its sense (2.221)

2.222 The **agreement** or disagreement of its [a picture's] sense with reality constitutes its truth or falsity

2.223 In order to tell whether a picture is true or false we must **compare** it with reality [emphasis added].

How does this comparison take place, according to Wittgenstein? Wittgenstein's answer to this question is the third major task of the *Tractatus*, an account of the connection between pictures, facts, thoughts, and propositions. The comparison between truth maker and truth bearer involves pictures qua human thoughts being compared with facts through the mediation of propositions. Wittgenstein claims that propositions mediate between facts (truth maker) and pictures (truth bearer): "For it is only by means of propositions that material properties are represented" (2.0231). Wittgenstein makes four moves to show how this works. First, he equates logical pictures with thoughts, "A logical picture of facts is a thought" (3). Second, he says that thoughts are expressible in ways that can be perceived by the senses in a proposition (3.1), and it is in propositions that "a thought can be expressed in such a way that the elements of the propositional sign correspond to the objects of the thought" (3.2). Third, Wittgenstein shows that the manner in which a thought is expressed (so that it corresponds with its object) occurs through a proposition. He states, "a thought is a proposition with a sense" (4). Fourth, he maintains that the thought can be expressed in a sense perceptible way. He states,

3.1 Thought finds expression that can be perceived by the senses.

3.11 We use the perceptible sign of a proposition (spoken or written, etc.) as a projection of a possible situation. The method of this projection is to think of the sense of the proposition.[8]

3.12 I call the sign with which we express a thought a propositional sign.—And a propositional sign in its projective relation to the world.

According to Wittgenstein, thought expresses itself in a way that can be perceived by the senses, and thought gets outside the mind into the physical world. Speech and writing are perceptible signs which signify a proposition. They project a thought or a picture, where pictures are understood as representations of possible states of affairs.

Wittgenstein elaborates his view of how the comparison between truth maker and truth bearer is made by describing the parts of a propositional sign. Propositional signs are constituted by the "determinate relation" of the words composing the sign (3.14). This determinate relation itself is a fact, part of the world. He states, "a propositional sign is a fact" (3.14). However, Wittgenstein is faced with questions of the following kind: Is this propositional sign "The green cat is on the mat" qua sense perceptible entity with six words standing in a certain sequential order, a fact in the same way that the state of affairs of (the green cat being on the mat) is a fact? Wittgenstein maintains that these two facts are equal in that they both express the sense of a proposition. He claims, "The essence of a propositional sign is very clearly seen if we imagine one composed of spatial objects (such as tables, chairs, and books) instead of written signs. Then the spatial arrangement of these things will express the sense of the proposition" (3.1431). By sense Wittgenstein means that which picture, thought, or proposition represents (i.e., a possible state of affairs). He emphasizes this by stating, "A proposition contains the form, but not the content of its sense" (3.13). By "content" he means "what is projected" (i.e., the state of affairs which is meant by the sense). Thus, the proposition presents the form, the possibility of a state of affairs in such a way that it is comparable with the state of affairs itself.

The role of "possibility" in this account of how the comparison between truth maker and truth bearer are made is very important. Propositions, like pictures and thoughts, involve possibilities of states of affairs. Wittgenstein makes it clear that a proposition does not include "what is projected," that is, the state of affairs itself. The sense of a proposition has merely "the possibility of expressing it [a state of affairs]" (3.13). He reminds his readers that the possibility of a states of affairs is not the state of affairs itself, but simply the form of that state of affairs. In order to determine if truth is present, the possibility of the state of affairs must be compared with the state of affairs itself. If there is a match between the possibility of the state of affairs (as expressed by the sense of a proposition) and the state of affairs itself, then the proposition is true.

By making these four moves, Wittgenstein tries to naturalize the relation of thought to the world by showing how the connection and the comparison between proposition and state of affairs is made. He summarizes his view of truth as the correspondence between thought and fact through propositions in the beginning of the fourth section of the *Tractatus*. He states,

> 4.05 Reality **is compared** with propositions
>
> 4.06 A proposition can be true or false only in virtue of **being a picture** of reality
>
> 4.062 For a proposition is true if we use it **to say that things stand in a certain way, and they do** [emphasis added].

Wittgenstein spends a good portion of the *Tractatus* describing one feature of the world, the logical structure of truth. He maintains that propositions represent the possibility of states of affairs and that the truth of propositions obtain when the possibility which the propositions represent are actual states of affairs. He focuses on the logical relations that obtain between elementary propositions and their possibility of being true or false, but he says little about exactly what the relationship is between proposition as the representation of a possible state of affairs and the state of affairs itself. This requires a more detailed ontology of universals and an account of intentionality, both of which the *Tractatus* lacks. Wittgenstein may think that such an account is unnecessary, or impossible, when he says, "What we cannot speak about we must pass over in silence" (7). However, without such an account, Wittgenstein's correspondence approach to truth is incomplete.

6.5 Andrew Newman[9]

A more recent analytic approach to the correspondence can be found in Andrew Newman's *The Correspondence Theory of Truth*. Newman defends a Russellian view of truth as correspondence with a focus on predicative beliefs. Perhaps it would be better to say that Newman's view is an early to mid-Russellian position, as Russell changed his mind on what truth is three ways: nature of the subject, the nature of relations, and the nature of truth bearers.[10] This is not, according to Newman, an "identity" theory of truth in that the relationship between the belief and reality are not numerically identical. Newman cites Alston's work on alethic realism as a way of showing the distinction between truth as numerical identity versus truth as correspondence of qualitative intentional content, where both the Russellian belief and reality "remain distinct entities" (p. 131).

Following Russell, Newman presents the formal hypothesis that "(S)Believes$R(a)(b)$" where S is the believing subject, R is a universal that binds the two (or more) particulars that obtain in parenthesis, and this entire three place relation "is an intentional relation" (p. 127). Newman states, "the universal R bonds first with the propositional attitude 'Believes' to give a three-place relation, namely, ( )BelievesR( )( ), which is then capable of bonding with three particulars, one of which is the subject" (p. 112). According to Newman, the object of belief is a particular, or a particular which stands in a certain relation to another particular. Thus, following Russell, a belief will be true when it corresponds to the "associated complex" and false otherwise.

The major question for Newman (and Russell and Wittgenstein) is: What is it about the belief and the object that gets them bonded together? If one is to maintain realism about one's correspondence theory of truth, the bonding relation cannot be due to the intentions of the agent doing the believing. There must be a kind of natural affinity between belief and object such that the universal R biding the particulars together exists independently of the agent's wishes. I want to suggest that realism about universals has the resources to allow for just such a natural affinity.[11] This natural affinity is a kind of "bridge between the mind and the world [which] resides in the way the mental properties that are concepts relate to, or have affinity for, other qualities—specifically, those that essentially qualify the objects which fall within the real or possible extension of the concept in question" (Willard 1999a). The same universal is present in the object and "intentionally" present in the belief had by the agent doing the believing. Thus, realism about universals helps shore up this gap in Newman's (and Russell's and Wittgenstein's) account of the bonding relation. We will examine Edmund Husserl's analysis of how this is possible in the next chapter.

6.6 Gerald Vision

Gerald Vision (Vision 2004) presents a view of truth as correspondence that is entirely linguistic. This view was put forward by Austin in his article "Truth" (Austin 1979). Vision in his very clearly written work presents an account of truth as correspondence along Austinian lines. His view can be summarized as follows:

(v) A statement Σ is true *if and only if* there is a sentence, S, tied descriptively to a type of state of affairs (henceforth SOA) such that

(1) Σ is made with S.

(2) There is a concrete SOA tokening that type to which S is descriptively tied.

(3) The token in (2) is relevant in the context (Vision p. 244).

This view can be expressed diagrammatically as follows:

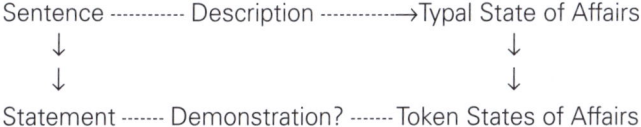

```
Sentence ----------- Description ------------→Typal State of Affairs
    ↓                                              ↓
    ↓                                              ↓
Statement ------- Demonstration? -------Token States of Affairs
```

There are two worries that I have about this understanding of truth as correspondence. The first is that it seems to leave out the key ontological nature of the relations that obtain between the relata. First, consider the first of the two vertical relations: the relation between sentence and statement. The relation here is not identity. These are two different things. This relation on Vision's view is one determined by "referential and deictic elements" (p. 240). While Vision doesn't claim to require a thoroughgoing theory of reference for his view to succeed, it seems that an account is needed of how a statement (which appears to be a particular instance of a sentence) relates to the more universal sentence.

Second, consider the relation between sentences and types of states of affairs. In this relation, types of states of affairs seem to be "abstract entities" (p. 231) and their relation to token states of affairs seems unexplained, other than a simple appeal to a brute type/token relation.

Third, consider the relation between sentences and types of states of affairs. This relation seems to be purely conventional as opposed to a natural relation. Vision states that there is "certitude that particular kinds of sentences are suited for use in, and the expression of, certain types of states of affairs" (p. 234). The question arises about the "suited for" relation here, which Vision claims might simply be a fundamental relation that is inexplicable in any greater detail. What is not articulated, however, is any notion of how the intentional content of a sentence and the properties of types of states of affairs relate in this "suited for" sort of way. What is lacking is the ontological apparatus to show how these relations obtain in such a way that they are not merely conventional, that is, stipulated by fiat, or reducible to pragmatic considerations. This quadratic alethic relation obtaining between sentences, types of states of affairs, token states of affairs, and statements isn't a manufactured relation, nor is it a causal relation. It seems to be a natural affinity relation that obtains just in case tokens of types of states of affairs are instantiated and statements (tokens?) of sentences (types?) are instantiated. But now there is the concern about what type of ontological commitments are able to handle at least the congruity, if not the possible correlation, that Vision claims obtains in his account. It seems to me that a realist account of the multiple instantiation of universals across different instances or instance types might help fill in this Austinian account.

6.7 Conclusion

In this section, I have sketched several of the more influential approaches to truth understood as correspondence. In each of these approaches, what seems lacking is the metaphysical apparatus needed to establish the correspondence relation. I believe that a thorough account of the way in which realism about properties or universals can make sense of the way in which a belief can correspond to the reality it is about. We turn now to Edmund Husserl's view on how this is possible.

7

Phenomenology of Correspondence

Chapter Outline

7.0 Introduction

I reach for my keys in my backpack to unlock my car. They are not there. I believe that I have left my keys on my desk. I return to my office (the secretary lets me in for the third time this semester), and

I look on my desk. I see my keys. I swipe them off the desk, mumble my apologies again to the secretary, call my wife to let her know I'll be late (again), and head to my car.

When I see that my keys are on my desk where I had believed them to be, I see the correspondence of my belief with reality. This is a common event. What is not as common as the event itself is a thorough analysis of the constituent parts of the event. Such an analysis of our beliefs matching reality is called a correspondence theory of truth. An analysis of the phenomena the "what it is like" to experience such an event can be called a phenomenological correspondence theory of truth.

In the previous chapter, we considered several attempts in the twentieth and twenty-first centuries to make sense of the correspondence relation in a correspondence theory of truth without such a phenomenology of truth. I argued that the difficulties for each of these views lay in the fact that without something to unify the truth maker and truth bearer, the relation of correspondence was empty. In this chapter, I present an exegetical sketch of one attempt to fulfill the relation of correspondence which relies on realism about universals by means of an analysis of the phenomenology of truth. This is the view maintained by Edmund Husserl in his *Logical Investigations*.

The main object of this section is to offer reasons for interpreting Edmund Husserl's view of truth, in his *Logical Investigations* (LI) (Husserl 1970), as a robust correspondence theory of truth which has an adequate account of the correspondence relation. In the first section, I present a brief commentary and overview of his view of truth. In the second section, I give a detailed exegetical description of his view of truth from the *Logical Investigations*. In this section, special emphasis will be given to the makers of truth, the bearers of truth, and the nature of the relation of correspondence between them. In brief, according to Husserl, truth bearers are thought-intentions, intentional mental states which have the possibility of corresponding to that which they are about. Truth makers are intuitions which are perceptual presentations of objects (or states of affairs) as they are in themselves. The correspondence relation between truth makers and truth bearers involves and depends upon an identity of instantiation of universals occurring in each. Husserl's entirely realist view of universals, his realism about the world, and his realist view of perception will be seen in the examination of passages from the *Logical Investigations*. In the final section of this chapter, I briefly indicate one recent attempt to continue seeing truth along Husserlian lines.

7.1 Overview and commentary of Husserl's view of truth

Any plausible correspondence theory of truth must make sense of the relation of correspondence by giving an account of its nature. Edmund Husserl gives such an account. Dallas Willard in his translator's introduction to Husserl's *Early Writings in the Philosophy of Logic and Mathematics* succinctly states where Husserl begins his analysis of truth as correspondence: "To understand what truth is, and what kind of correlations it involves, we must look at cases where we can intuitively encounter the agreement between representation and object" (Husserl 1994, p. XLIV). Instances of truth as correspondence can be found by us as they present themselves in our experiences. According to Husserl, it is in these experienced instances of the relation of correspondence that the relation of correspondence can be analyzed adequately.

Willard states, and it will be shown below, that according to Husserl, "Truth is a relationship which shows up between consciousness and its objectivity when the objectivity is found to be as it is thought to be. It is an adequation with the 'thing itself'" (p. XLIV). Truth as correspondence amounts to a "relation between the Ideal constituents of acts of consciousness—propositions or judgments in the logical sense—and what those propositions are inherently about, regardless of whether or not they are ever actually thought by, or occur to, anyone" (p. XLIV).

Husserl maintains that the truth bearers in the correspondence relation are propositions. Willard explains that Husserl takes propositions to be abstract, complex referential qualities, which have the same ontological status as universals on a realist metaphysics; but, unlike universals, propositions can only be instantiated in minds. Husserl's view of the truth makers in the relation of correspondence is part and parcel of his ontological realist metaphysics.[1] Husserl indicates that the relation between propositions and acts of judgment is similar to the relation between redness qua universal and physical individuals which instantiate the same red color (see Willard 1984, pp. 181–185). Just as there is an identity between a universal and the universal instanced in an object, so too there is an identity between the proposition and its instance in an act of consciousness, and between the proposition and the object which it is about.

Husserl claims that propositions, and derivatively statements and sentences, are the bearers of truth. Logicians can make truth claims of particular instances of propositions when instanced in particular sentences or statements made by someone, but their truth claims are not dependent on the existence of particular sentences or statements. Willard indicates that Husserl's view of propositions as complex referential qualities makes sense of this, since "propositions are not particular acts of thought, but are complex, referential characteristics or qualities *of* such acts" (Willard 1984, p. 184). These qualities have various determinations which include truth and falsity and conditions of truth and falsity. When a person's thoughts instantiate a proposition, the determinations of the propositions enter into concrete acts of thinking. This analysis of how truth claims are made about particular instances of propositions indicates that truth claims are not dependent on individual acts of speech or thought, but are made of the universals instanced in particular acts. Truth as correspondence, while it may involve a relation between particular acts of thought and objects, is not dependent on those particular acts, but is dependent on the existence of the propositions which instance themselves in those acts.

According to Husserl, thought-intentions which are propositions instanced in thought (as intentional mental states which have the possibility of corresponding to that which they are about) are the primary bearers of truth. Intuitions which are perceptual presentations of objects (or states of affairs) as they are in themselves are the makers of truth. As will be discussed below, Husserl is careful to avoid the problems that arise with this relation by making a clear distinction between (i) the object, (ii) the perception of the object, (iii) the judgment of the object, (iv) the relation of correspondence between the perception and the judgment, and (v) the subject's awareness of the object, the perception, the judgment, and the relation of correspondence.

In a section entitled "The Idea of Truth" of his unpublished essay "Intentional Objects" (1894), Husserl claims that object and judgment are distinct, that an object is not literally *in* the truths about it, and he claims that an object and truths about it are also distinct. He states that "truth is something Ideal, supra-temporal, whereas the object quite well can be something real" (Husserl 1994, p. 380). Although they are distinct, there is a connection of identity of universals between object and object as thought in which truth is experienced. This identity appears in an act of fulfillment wherein an object of experience is seen to be as it has been thought to be. One experiences a coincidence of instances of universals instanced in the object and the object as thought. In the experience of the object and the experience of the object as thought, there is a fulfilled intuition (a thought fulfilled by an object). This is a coincidence or correspondence between object and intuition in virtue of the identity of the universal with itself in its instances (Husserl 1994, pp. 384–385).

Husserl's view of truth as a correspondence relation involves (but is not the same as) a relation of identity. This relation is similar to the relation of identity between different instances of the same universal. Truth just is the relation that obtains between a proposition taken as a complex referential quality or universal (truth bearer), and the object which this proposition is about (truth maker).[2] There are three things involved in this sort of correspondence theory of truth. There is (i) the proposition qua complex referential quality/universal, (ii) an object instantiating the universals of the proposition, and (iii) someone's particular thought\statement\sentence about the object. For Husserl, truth is always correspondence between (i) and (ii). Item (iii) in this list enters into consideration when one experiences truth, or makes a truth claim about some particular proposition and its relation to some object. Let us turn to the passages in the *Logical Investigations* in which Husserl presents his version of truth as correspondence.

7.1.1 *Truth is non-relative and absolute*

In his *Logical Investigations* in the "Prolegomena to Pure Logic" Husserl argues against psychologism, the view that the principles of logic are psychological (i.e., they are descriptive of the mind's operations). In his criticism of psychologism, he argues against anthropologism, the view that truth is relative to species. In his attack on this form of relativism, Husserl says something positive about the nature of truth. Husserl claims,

> What is true is absolutely, intrinsically true: truth is one and the same, whether men or non-men, angels or gods apprehend and judge it. Logical laws speak of truth in this ideal unity, set over against the real multiplicity of races, individuals and experiences, and it is of this ideal unity that we all speak when we are not confused by relativism.
>
> (p. 140)

There are a few things that are important in this quotation. First, note Husserl's idea that whatever it may be that is true *is* true both absolutely and intrinsically. By "absolute" Husserl implies that whatever it is that turns out to *be* true has truth fully present within it. Whatever the bearer of truth might be, if any truth bearer is true, it is true because of what it is in and of itself. The bearers of truth have within themselves what it takes to be made true by truth makers. By "intrinsic" he means both that what is true is free from dependence of anything outside of itself (e.g., human minds). Whatever *is* true is itself not truth. Rather, whatever *is* true is an instance of truth. Second, note that truth is not relative. Truth is "one and the same" for all intelligent beings. Third, Husserl appeals to logical laws as examples of how truth is expressed as an "ideal unity." By "ideal" he means existing as an Idea, a Platonic form. By "unity" he means that truth is an ontologically independent entity which is a unified whole, and not a mere conglomeration of other Ideas meshed by a mind into a "whole." This ideal unity is what allows there to be and what is found in a multiplicity of experiences. The laws of logic are examples of an ideal unity across a multiplicity of minds. Logical truths can be instanced in (and in turn govern or constrain) many different thought processes, or processes of reasoning.

7.1.2 *Truth as both a-temporal and temporal*

Husserl also claims that truth itself is a-temporal, although "a" truth with regard to some fact is temporally determined (p. 141).

Is Husserl's view that a truth with regard to a fact is temporally determined, mistaken? Laws of logic or mathematics are facts, but they are a-temporal, and thus, truths about them would also be a-temporal. Perhaps Husserl is referring only to temporally determined facts. Indeed, facts according to Husserl may just be the kind of things which exist temporally, since they exist individually.

7.1.3 *Truth as neither cause nor effect*

Husserl states that truths and truth itself are not causes or effects (p. 141). This is evident in the distinction between the content and the act of judgment. He indicates that just as there is a distinction between the content and the act of a judgment, there is also a distinction between a "true judgment, as the correct judgment in accordance with truth, with the *truth* of this judgment or with the true content of judgment. My act of judging that $2 \times 2 = 4$ is no doubt causally determined, but this is not true of the truth $2 \times 2 = 4$" (p. 142). Truth itself is that which is *in* individual truths, and individual truths are dependent (as truths) upon the states of affairs or facts which they are about.

The example he provides shows what Husserl means by truth and truths not being causes or effects. The act of judgment that $2 \times 2 = 4$ is contrasted with the truth $2 \times 2 = 4$. The truth of the mathematical statement is independent from the judgment of the content of the statement. The individual act of judgment may be the cause of other effects, or the effect of some other judgment, but the truth itself of what is judged is itself neither a cause nor an effect. This places Husserl's view of truth outside the realm of natural causation.

7.1.4 *Truth as existence*

Husserl claims that there is a deep connection between truth and the existence of the world, where "world" includes anything that exists, including logical truths. He states, "The relativity of truth entails the relativity of cosmic existence." The relativist's claim that truth is relative to the human species implies the relativity of the nature (structure or existence) of the world to the human species. [3] However, and this shows the absurdity of the view, the human species is itself a part of the world. Husserl argues, "For the world is merely the unified objective totality corresponding to, and inseparable from, the ideal system of all factual truth" (p. 143).

Husserl betrays a strong dualism here. There are two things which correspond and are inseparable: the world qua unified objective totality corresponds to and is inseparable from "the ideal system of all factual truth." The key phrases here are "unified objective totality" and "ideal system of all factual truth." By "ideal system of all factual truth," Husserl means the ideal range of universals/forms which are logically possible as instances in objects. He calls this a system, because it is a range of ideal universals/forms which inform everything in the world. This range of universals/forms is what makes things in the world to be as they are. Husserl seems to say the world is the concrete system of factual truth and corresponds to and is inseparable from a range of universals which is the ideal system of factual truth. This is essentially a dualism of properties along Platonic lines; universals (Ideas in Husserl's terminology) exist separately and independently of the things which have them, and in themselves constitute a unified system of truth.

7.1.5 Truth as idea

In his criticism of Sigwart's psychologism, Husserl also touches on Sigwart's view of truth. In doing so, Husserl puts forth a positive claim of the nature of truth, claiming:

> "Truth … is eternal," or better put, it is an Idea, and so beyond time … truth is not a phenomenon among phenomena, but is the experience on that totally different sense in which a universal, an idea, is an experience. We are conscious of truth, as we are in general conscious of a Species, e.g. of the Colour Red.
>
> (p. 148)

He is claiming here that truth *simpliciter* is an Idea.[4] Truth as a universal can be analyzed and experienced by us when it is instantiated. This is analogous to experiences of the universal Red in its various instances. He claims that truth is apprehended, but when it is apprehended, it is not the experience of apprehending truth, as when truth comes to mind. Rather, truth is experienced or made conscious to us in the same way as the Species Red is present in an experience of a red object. The experience itself is not Red, but Red is present in the experience.

Husserl illustrates how truth is like any other Idea. He asks us to consider a perception of a red object. He describes the parts of this experience as follows. First, there is the red object which has as one of its parts a "non-independent moment of red, an instance of Redness" (p. 149) which is as individual as the object itself. Second, there is Redness itself, an "ideal unity" which does not come into being or pass away. When we apprehend the object, we apprehend the individual instance of redness, but we are able through the instance to refer to the Species (Idea) Redness. If this is done with several red objects, we can then apprehend the identity of these ideal unities as the same Species present in each instance.

Consider the relation of this to the nature of truth. If truth is understood as the adequation of thing and intellect, as Husserl (and Thomas Aquinas) maintains, then one can experience an instance of truth. The individual adequation of thing and intellect is an instance of truth, or rather truth is present in the adequation. Husserl's claim is that truth is an Idea and functions in the same way. He states, "like any other Idea it is given in an act of Ideation based upon an intuition [a perceptual presentation of an object]" (p. 149). One is able to see the idea of truth in an act of thinking about that which instances the idea. Once one sees various instances of truth in one's acts of thinking, one can see the unity and identity of truth itself, over against individual instances of truth qua universal.

Husserl claims that truth itself is independent from its instances, and is what informs all instances of adequation. It is in this sense that truth is like a universal. It is *in* many instances, but is *independent* of all of them. Husserl maintains that for any statement, "it is the truth that ...," even if there were no minds that could see this truth, or see the nature of truth in particular, "each truth, however, remains in itself what it is, it retains its ideal being: it does not hang somewhere in the void, but is a case of validity in the timeless realm of Ideas" (p. 149).[5] Thus, an instance of truth can be understood as the adequation of thing and intellect, but truth itself is an ideal possibility of the adequation of thing and intellect, and exists logically prior to any mind with which it might be instanced in an act of adequation.

7.1.6 Truth as independent

In his criticism of B. Erdmann's psychologism and relativism, Husserl argues against the psychologistic idea that truth "has its seat in knowledge, and that knowledge as a mental experience is of course subject to psychological laws" (p. 164). Husserl points out that knowledge and error are not interchangeable based on mere changes in psychological facts. For example, red will always be a color and not a tone. He indicates that persons may always believe something false which is true, or believe something true which is false. However, "this would leave truth and falsehood intrinsically unaffected: they are essentially properties of the contents of such judgments, not of judgments as acts. They pertain to such contents even if no one recognizes their presence" (p. 165). By properties of contents of such judgments he is referring to the universals that make up the range of instances of those universals in objects which are mind independent.

7.1.7 Truth as correspondence

The mind-independent nature of truth is also shown in his analysis of the nature of logic and its relation to various sciences. Husserl maintains that science, when considered with respect to what it teaches, has a certain content embodied in statements which are either true or false. "What each statement states is—in the ideal case—a truth" (p. 173). This is another example of Husserl's holding to truth as independent of the human mind and as a form of correspondence. In this case the correspondence is between the content of a statement (truth bearer) and that object or state of affairs to which a statement refers (truth maker).[6]

In Husserl's criticism of the view that "all truth lies in our judgments" (p. 189), the notion of truth as correspondence emerges. Husserl maintains that the propositions P1: "A is true" and P2: "It is possible for anyone to judge A to be true in an inwardly evident manner" are related, he denies P1 and P2 state the same thing. P1 does not say anything about "anyone's judgment, [nor] even about judgments of anyone in general" (p. 190). P2 is dependent upon P1; according to Husserl, there is a dependency of the inward evidence of a judgment upon *ideal* conditions. He states,

> Each truth stands as an ideal unity over against an endless, unbounded possibility of correct statements which have its form and its matter in common. Each actual judgment which belongs to this ideal manifold, will fulfill, either in its mere form or in its matter, the ideal conditions for its own possible inward evidence. The laws of pure logic are truths rooted in the concept of truth, and in concepts essentially related to this concept.
>
> (p. 192)

Several things are noteworthy in this quotation. First, an individual truth, as presented in P1, is an ideal unity. By ideal Husserl means an abstract form, like a number or universal. By unity, Husserl means that an individual truth is a range of universals that are internally related together forming a complete whole. Each truth can be instanced in an unlimited number of correct statements by various individuals, and when so instanced has the truth's form (the universals of which the truth is composed) and matter (that which the truth is about) in common. When a judgment is made, it belongs to this ideal manifold in the sense that either its form or matter has instanced in it (in an intentional way) the universals of which the truth is composed.

Second, it is important to recognize that Husserl's main concern in this passage is a discussion of the nature of the laws of logic. On his view, the laws of logic follow the general pattern of truth as an ideal unity just described. A particular logical law exists apart from being thought of or instanced in any logical act of thought. However, when it is instanced, the act of thought has instanced in it the range of universals that are found in the particular law of logic; a law of logic is a truth, a logically possible range of universals, an ideal unity.

This particular Platonic view of truths of logical laws is superior to both coherence and pragmatic views of truth. For the coherentist, a logical law is true only due to its relation to other logical laws. Yet, there does not seem to be a way to make sense of deductive validity where one maintains that if the premises of a deduction were true, then the conclusion of an argument would necessarily be true. Validity (as well as soundness) cannot be grounded in coherence. Pragmatism (in its stronger forms) would require that logical laws exist due to our interests or are true only because of pragmatic principles. Husserl's Platonic view of logical laws preserves the objectivity and the normativity of logic.

This brief account presents insight into Husserl's understanding of truth as correspondence. In the passage above he clearly indicates that a truth (which involves propositions and facts as will be discussed below), has the possibility of being instanced in some act of thought. For example, the laws of logic are true apart from individual minds in a unique way. If a law of logic exists, it does so in propositional form, and it has a content which is descriptive of one part of reality namely, the ideal unity of logical forms. This law can be true (i.e., correspond with facts) even if minds are needed to instantiate the facts with which the law *qua* proposition corresponds.

Husserl's account of truth implies, for two reasons, that the existence of human minds is irrelevant for the existence of truth as an ideal unity.[7] First, each ideal logical law carries with it an adequate description of reality in sort of a subjunctive sense, "if there were instances of logical thoughts then this law would govern/regulate them." Second, and more strongly, a proposition itself is about the realm of logic. If we assume that there is a logically possible totality of ideas (forms/propositions) which can be instanced in human minds but exists independently of human minds, then the laws of logic govern the possible relationships among all ideas (forms/propositions) which have ideally similar content. For example, the logical law of non-contradiction is an idea (form or proposition) about other logical propositions, and as a proposition about other propositions it governs the possible relationships among all propositions. Husserl maintains the first reason, but implies the stronger second reason. Truths, especially truths and laws of logic, exist independently of human minds and govern the ideal realm of propositions. These propositions with their logical laws can be instanced in human minds, and as instances of formal laws, they govern the instances in the same way that they govern the ideal entities. It is because they govern the formal (ideal) realm that they govern instances of these forms.[8]

7.1.8 *Truth and the real/ideal distinction*

Husserl claims that the distinction between the real and the ideal is *the* fundamental distinction in epistemology. Our understanding of this distinction rests on our understanding between real and ideal theories of inner evidence which Husserl claims are dependent on our concepts of inner evidence and truth (p. 194). Husserl claims that inner evidence "is nothing but the *experience* of truth" (p. 194). He states, "Truth is of course only experienced in the sense in which something ideal can be an experience in a real act." Stated in another way, " *Truth is an Idea, whose particular case is an actual experience in the inwardly evident judgment*" (p. 194). He continues, "Inner evidence is called a seeing, a grasping of the self-given (true) state of affairs … of the truth" (p. 195). Thus, truth exists independently of human cognition, according to Husserl, but is instanced in human cognition. It is both real (immanent in experience) and ideal (transcendent from) human experience.[9]

This occurs, according to Husserl, in the following way: " *The experience of the agreement* between meaning and what is itself present, meant, between the actual *sense of an assertion* and the self-given *state of affairs*, is inward evidence: the *Idea* of this agreement is truth, whose ideality is also its objectivity" (p. 195). In this quotation, Husserl elaborates on what has been said above. Truth is correspondence between ideal propositions and the objective realities which instance the content of those ideal propositions. Human minds can instance this relation when they apprehend the experience of agreement between the "sense of an assertion" and the "state of affairs." Any instance of this in human experience is an instance of the formal Idea of truth. The last phrase of this quotation is profound. The ideality of truth is also its objectivity. Husserl means by this, first and foremost that truth is an idea, but as an idea it is objective and not subjective. All ideas are such that they exist apart from human cognition, although they can be instanced in human cognition. Truth's ideality is its objectivity. If all ideas are objective, and truth is an idea, then truth is objective. The ideality of truth is what makes truth objective and keeps truth from sliding into the abyss of relativism.

7.1.9 *Truth and knowledge as fulfillment*

In this section, I will clarify more precisely Husserl's understanding of the exact nature of the correspondence relation along with the specifics of the relation itself. In his introduction to Investigation VI "Objectifying Intentions and their Fulfillments: Knowledge as a Synthesis of Fulfillment and Its Gradations," Husserl attempts to make a phenomenological characterization of knowledge as the fulfillment of an intuition (a mental state derived by seeing an object) by an intention (a concept in the mind directed toward some object) which in its final form is "being in the sense of truth, *correspondence* rightly understood, the *adaequatio rei ad intellectus*. This *adaequatio* is itself given, to be directly seized and gazed upon" (p. 670).

Husserl discusses the connection between knowledge and truth in the fifth chapter of Investigation VI. He summarizes his account of fulfillment in which an intention is completely and entirely fulfilled. He states,

> The intuitive substance of this last fulfillment is the absolute sum of possible fullness; the intuitive representative is the object itself, as it is in itself. Where a presentative intention has achieved its last fulfillment, the genuine *adaequatio rei et intellectus* has been brought about. *The object is actually present or given, and present as just what we have intended it*; no partial intention remains implicit and still lacking fulfillment.
>
> (p. 762)

In this quotation Husserl presents a clear description of what truth as correspondence actually means. He does three things. First, he describes the truth bearer. Second, he describes the truth maker, and third, he states the nature of the correspondence relation between truth bearer and truth maker.

First, what are the items of correspondence according to Husserl? The truth bearer is a thought-intention, a mental state which has the possibility of corresponding to that which it is about. In the quotation above the intellectus is the thought-intention, the intention of meaning directed outwards toward some object. The intentional state is fulfilled, using Husserl's terminology (or adequated, using Thomas Aquinas' term) by an intuition (e.g., a direct perceptual experience).

Second, the truth maker is an intuition which is a perceptual presentation of an object as it is in itself. Husserl calls this the *rei* in the quotation above. The thing itself is present in an intuition, an act of seeing directly the object as it is in itself.[10] Husserl maintains that when one is presented with an object, one perceives objects directly. He states, "when we have a presentation, or judgment about a horse, it is a horse, not our sensation of the moment, that is presented and judged about" (p. 382). This is much different than the modern "way of ideas" which runs from Descartes through Kant and beyond. That view maintains that what we are aware of in our acts of awareness are ideas and not the things themselves. An adequate correspondence view, one that really connects mind and world, thought and experience can only work on a realist view such as Husserl develops.

Third, by *adequatio* in the quotation above, Husserl means the relation of correspondence which he calls fulfillment. Truth as *adequatio* or fulfillment or correspondence between thing and intellect occurs in such a way that we can see the match, as a door fits its frame, between thought-intention and intuition. The *adequatio* is realized when "the object meant is in the strict sense *given* in our intuition, and given as just what we think and call it" (p. 762). This is the clearest descriptive account of correspondence as the adequation of thing and intellect which Husserl provides.[11]

It is important to recognize that on Husserl's account, there is a deep connection between an account of truth and an account of perception. An account of perception is needed to make clear how a thing is related to the intellect. If what we perceive are not things as they are in themselves; if what we perceive are sense data or sensations, or ideas which merely represent things as they are, or somehow cut us off from things as they are, then the notion of truth of adequation of thing and intellect is dead in the water. This notion of truth would have to be reformulated to be adequation of percept and intellect.

Husserl makes it clear that his account of perception fits with his view of truth as adequation of thing and intellect. He relies on a direct realist account of perception, a view in which it is maintained that we perceive objects and their properties and not sense data or sense perceptions.[12] When we are presented with that which the thought-intention is about, we are directly presented with an intuition, a direct looking at, an immediate seeing into the essence and properties of the thing intuited. He states that thought, or as indicated above, thought-intention "aims at a thing, and it hits its mark, or does not hit it, according as it agrees or does not agree in a certain way with perception" (p. 764).

Husserl's view of the hitting the mark (adequation) of intellect and thing rests upon his account of perception. Husserl states, "The concept of verification relates exclusively *to assertive acts in relation to their assertive fulfillment*, and ultimately to their *fulfillment through percepts*" (p. 765). By "assertive acts," Husserl simply means acts of thought-intentions or meanings. Husserl means by "assertive fulfillment" the universals/ideas that are needed to fulfill a specific thought-intention. Verification (seeing truth) occurs when an individual identifies their assertive act with a percept. A percept is a direct presentation of a thing as it is in itself.

This fulfillment is itself an act in which an object is "given, and given as it is meant, and made one with our meaning-reference [thought-intention]" (p. 765). Husserl calls this ultimate fulfillment "self-evidence" and an act of "identification." "It is an objectifying act, its objective correlate being called *being in the sense of truth*, or simply *truth*" (p. 765). By "objectifying act" Husserl means an act which instantiates or is an instance of, something objective (e.g., finding my keys where I believed I left them). The act of fulfillment, adequation of thing and intellect, instantiates "an objective correlate" which Husserl calls "being in the sense of truth, or simply truth." It is interesting that Husserl would call these acts of fulfillment "objectifying." He goes beyond the notion that truth is only adequation of thing and intellect in this description of fulfillment. Truth seems to be something that is found *in* acts of fulfillment but exists apart from them. Truth can be present in an objectifying act of fulfillment because truth is a form of being that exists apart from individual objectifying acts.

7.1.10 *Four concepts of truth*

At the close of Chapter 5, "The Ideal of Adequation: Self Evidence and Truth" in Investigation VI, Husserl makes a distinction between four different conceptual senses of truth, or four different ways of describing truth as the adequation of thing and intellect.

i. Truth as the correlate of an identifying act is a *state of affairs*, as the correlate of a coincident identity it is an *identity: the full agreement* of what is meant with what is *given as such.*

(p. 765).

In the first sense, truth is found in the identifying acts themselves. It is the state of affairs of the act of identification. In the act of identification it is also the identity itself, the agreement as such. This is truth instantiated in human acts of identification and fulfillment. In this sense, truth is most literally adequation of thing and intellect. Truth is the act of adequation itself (finding my keys).

ii. Truth is also "the *ideal relationship* which obtains in the unity of coincidence which we defined as self-evidence, *among the epistemic essences of the coinciding acts.* Truth in *this* sense is the Idea which belongs to the act-form: *the epistemic essence interpreted as the ideal essence of the empirically contingent act of self-evidence, the Idea of absolute adequation as such.*"

(p. 766)

In this second sense, truth is an ideal relationship. Truth in its ideal (formal) sense like other universals (e.g., redness) can be instantiated in various things. The kinds of things in which truth in the ideal sense can be instantiated are limited to minds. Just as the universal, red can be instantiated in various red objects, so too, truth qua universal can be instantiated in various identifying mental acts.

The Idea (form/universal) of truth is instantiated in an act of coincidence or fulfillment of a thought-intention by an intuition. Both a thought-intention (e.g., a belief that my keys are on my desk) and an intuition (the experience of seeing my keys being on my desk) have epistemic essences; they have content and are about something. As individuals had by some mind, the content of the thought-intention and the intuition are themselves intentional instances of universals. The Idea of truth is instantiated in an act when the universals instanced in both the thought-intention and intuition are fulfilled, coincide, or correspond. This idea/universal can be instanced in multiple minds as well. We can each have the same truth present across multiple intellects.

In the first sense above, truth is understood as the act of adequation of the instances of universals with one another; in this second sense, truth is understood as a universal or form of those instances of adequation. Just as we might have three of the same doors that fit three of the same door frames, the fitting of each door to its frame is analogous to truth in sense one above, the act of identification of coincidence. Using this analogy to express the second sense of truth, the three doors each instantiate the same universal (or group of universals) as do the frames. Each act of fitting of door to frame also instantiates the universal "fitting-of-door-to-frame," and in this sense, the fit can be understood in its universal sense apart from the individual fittings in which it is instantiated. The same can be said of truth.

iii. In regards to the third sense of truth, Husserl states,

> We … experience … *the object given in the manner of the object meant*…This object can also be called … truth, the truth insofar as it is here not experienced as in the merely adequate percept, but as the ideal fullness for an intention, as that which makes an intention true (or as the ideal fullness for the intention's *specific* epistemic essence).
>
> (p. 766)

Truth in the third sense can be understood as the experience of the object *qua* intuition fulfilling the thought-intention (the experience of finding my keys). This is the experience of "the object given in the manner of the object meant," the adequation of thing and intellect. Husserl does two things here. First, he maintains that truth can be experienced. Second, he makes truth objective (rather than subjective or relative) as "the ideal fullness for an intention, as that which makes an intention true." What makes intentions true are the objects which have various properties that enter into acts of perception and are intuited by the subject perceiving and then matched, identified, and adequated, corresponding with a thought-intention. Husserl points out twofold features of truth here as both subjectively experienced and objectively "experience-able."

iv. Truth as the "*rightness of our* intention (and especially that of our judgment), its adequacy to its true object, or the *rightness of the intentions's epistemic essence in specie.*"

(p. 766)

In sense three, Husserl emphasizes the objective aspect of truth as the pointing inward of an object qua intuition toward a thought-intention. On the fourth notion of truth, Husserl emphasizes the subjective aspect of truth, the direction of intention outward toward its object. However, he is careful to keep hold of the objective aspect of intention. The intention itself contains instances of various universals, and when it is fulfilled by an object there is a match between the universals of the object and the intention. This rightness of an intention, a judgment's "epistemic essence in specie," can be understood both as the rightness or fit of the intention, an instance or instances of universals, or as the rightness of the universals themselves insofar as the same universals are present in the intention and its true object.

7.1.11 *Summary*

Husserl's view of truth as correspondence has an objective part (intuition) and a subjective part (thought-intention). However, the emphasis is on the objective side. Husserl maintains that when truth is instantiated in an act of fulfillment, that act itself becomes an objective reality which can be understood, evaluated, and analyzed. It is from a phenomenological investigation of the aspects of this act that Husserl derives his account of truth. Dallas Willard concisely summarizes this form of objectivity of Husserl's view in the *Logical Investigations*.

Whenever intention and intuition come together in that ideally perfect synthesis of fulfillment constituting re-cognition—in the *Evidenz* which is the highest form of fulfillment (533)—a *new* object or objectivity appears, which is neither that of the mere intention or that of the intuition, taken by itself. This new objective correlate is *being in the sense of truth*, one of the many concepts of truth rooted in the structure of fulfillment. (765f) The *adequatio* or "correspondence" of concept to intuition is "directly seized and gazed upon." (670; cf. 762)

                                                   (Willard 1984, pp. 228–229)

Truth is objective, independent from human experience but can be fully known in our ordinary experiences. These experiences can serve as the point of departure for our study and knowledge of truth.

7.2 Challenges for Husserlian phenomenology

There are at least two challenges which may militate against Husserl's view of truth as correspondence, or indeed any view constructed along Husserlian lines. First, if direct realism about perception fails, it does not seem clear to me at all how Husserl's view of truth as adequation of thing and intellect could proceed. If we do not have access to things as they are in themselves, then there can be no adequation of thing and intellect. The most we could hope for would be adequation of *percept* and intellect. This might be a sort of indirect or mediated realism about truth, but it would cut us off substantially from truth about the way the world *is* independent of our perceptions of it. In fact, if direct perceptual realism fails, then we cannot begin (as I have tried to do in this book) with our commonsense experiences of finding things as we have thought them to be. The best we could do is merely postulate (maybe in a Kantian fashion as the result of his antinomies) that we should *hope* for the truth, but not that we can *see* the truth.

Second, if a general defense of realism about universals (whether Platonic or Aristotelian) cannot be sustained, then Husserl's view (and I would argue, any correspondence view) will also fail. The unity of truth bearer and truth maker in the correspondence relation can only be sustained if there is something in each relata which is identical to the other. Husserl argues that this unity is generated by the identity of a universal instanced in each relata (albeit intentionally in a concept and actually in the world). If there are no universals (i.e., if some form of nominalism were true), then correspondence views of truth will fail as well. We will return to this point in the next chapter.

7.3 A recent Husserlian approach[13]

Richard Fumerton in *Realism and the Correspondence Theory of Truth* presents a realistic analysis of the correspondence relation along Husserlian lines. His view involves a representational account of intentional states. Fumerton states, "The capacity to represent some feature of the world just is the capacity to correspond to some feature of the world" (Fumerton 2002, p. 42).

Fumerton presents a formalization of this view. The formalization of this relation involves existential quantification and the correspondence relation: "(t) t is true *iff* there exists some x such that t C x" (p. 41). Fumerton's correspondence relation, he argues, is not causal; rather it is a fundamental un-analyzable relation that is simply part of the fabric of the world. He suggests the trivial and simple example that correspondence is the relation that obtains between "my belief that I am in pain and my pain" (p. 47).

Again, following Husserl, Fumerton rests much of his description of the correspondence relation on the phenomenology of experiences. He states, "Without phenomenology there is no argument for dualism, and without dualism the idea that there are states that have the capacity to represent just in virtue of their intrinsic character truly is a mysterious view" (p. 49). This leads him to clarify the notion of truth involving intentionality in the following formalization: "s believes truly that P *iff* 'P*'s and there exists an x such that 'P' C x" (p. 49) [P = "the property of thinking *about p*", P* = an intentional belief state (pp. 49–50)].

It is the intentional belief state that is the "sui generis" lynchpin for Fumerton's realistic correspondence account of truth. I quote Fumerton at length here to see his general point:

> In being acquainted with the thought that one is in pain, and the pain itself one also finds oneself acquainted with the relation of correspondence holding between the thought and the pain. It is precisely for this reason that one doesn't need to infer the truth of the proposition that one is in pain from some other proposition … one has "before" consciousness both truth bearers (thoughts) and truth makers (facts). It is through such acts of acquaintance that

we can "ostend," so to speak, the critical properties and relations the ideas of which are the conceptual atoms of the above account of truth and falsehood. (p. 52)

Fumerton is echoing Edmund Husserl's general account of how exactly an intentional mental state can stand in a correspondence relation to something that exists. Instances of truth as correspondence can be found by us as they present themselves in our experiences. According to Husserl, it is in these experienced instances of the relation of correspondence that truth can be analyzed adequately in terms of truth bearers, truth makers, and the correspondence relation between them.

However, it seems to me that the only way that there can be any sort of intentional state between an object and a mental state is if there is some sort of identity between the two; some third thing is needed to bridge the gap between the mind and the world such that there is correspondence between them. Husserl's account of Ideas (understood along Platonic or possibly Aristotelian lines) and universals do just that. When I have an intentional mental state (belief, thought, sentence, statement, etc.) I have in my mind a mental state that is directed toward a possible instance of a universal. When an object instantiates the universals which are intended in my beliefs, there is an automatic correspondence between belief and object, linked through the universals present (albeit in different senses) in each member of the correspondence relation. Without realism about universals (i.e., properties, forms, ideas, etc.), Fumerton's correspondence relation cannot adequately connect the relata in the correspondence relation.

7.4 Conclusion

I conclude this chapter with two suggestions. First, a defender of a realistic correspondence theory of truth using metaphysical realism about universals needs to be able to show how non-Platonic realist accounts of universals (e.g., nominalism or idealism) cannot make sense of the natural affinity between the members of the correspondence relation. This would consist in a sort of argument by elimination, showing that metaphysical realism about universals has greater problem solving capacity than its rivals. Second, defenders of the position I maintain here should also explore how commonsense approaches to truth as correspondence starting from particular cases of truth (e.g., I know what it is like to find the book in the bookstore, as I thought it to be) can be used as paradigmatic and simple units of analysis for a robust realist correspondence theory of truth. We simply begin with case of correspondence with which we are already familiar and analyze outward an account which utilizes the resources of metaphysical realism about universals. We will examine this further in the following chapter.

8

Realism and Common Sense

8.0 Introduction

I reach for my keys in my backpack to unlock my car. They are not there. I believe that I have left my keys on my desk. I return to my office (the secretary lets me in for the third time this semester), and I look on my desk. I see my keys. I swipe them off the desk, mumble my apologies again to the secretary, call my wife to let her know I'll be late (again), and head to my car.

When I see that my keys are on my desk where I had believed them to be, I see the correspondence of my belief with reality. This is a common event. This common event can be understood best by means of ideas from St. Thomas Aquinas, Edmund Husserl, a defense of realism about universals, and a patient phenomenological analysis of truth in our common sense.

In this chapter, I want to introduce into the discussion the idea of truth as adequation of thing and intellect defended by

St. Thomas Aquinas. First, I argue that metaphysics, understood as ontology or the study of being qua being, requires a logically coextensive theory of truth; truth requires metaphysics. Second, I argue that the only possible account of truth which can be logically coextensive with any possible metaphysics, whether monistic or dualistic, is the correspondence theory of truth. Third, I argue that only correspondence theories which are metaphysically robust can serve as the basis of metaphysics. In particular, I argue that only correspondence theories which rely upon a realistic understanding of universals (e.g., Platonism) can serve adequately as the basis of an epistemology of metaphysics. Fourth, I argue that a correspondence theory based upon realism about universals is itself an instance of the ultimate nature of reality. Seeing truth (in both speculative philosophy and our commonsense everyday experiences) points us to metaphysics and beyond.

8.1 Metaphysics

In his *Disputed Questions on Truth*, Aquinas begins his reply in the first article "What is Truth?" by quoting Avicenna saying, "that which the intellect first conceives as…the most evident…is being" (Aquinas 1952). Epistemology, at least in the sense of that which is *evident* to the intellect, begins with ontology (metaphysics).[1] As our intellects come to develop their epistemologies, their understandings of their own capacities and faculties of knowledge, they see that contained within being as such, there are modes of being, one of which is truth.

In order to come to see that being contains truth within itself as a mode of being, we should first begin with a distinction in types of conceiving. "To conceive" can be understood in at least two ways. First, we can conceive of that which is not real and has no being apart from the act of conceiving (that which instantiates no properties, e.g., to conceive of the golden mountain), and we can conceive of what is real and has being apart from the act of conceiving (that which instantiates properties, e.g., my golden ring). In one way, that which is most evident to the intellect is being of both a conceiving of that which is not real and that which is real. For in both acts of conceiving the intellect has before it the being of the conception, as well as the being of the conceiver. However, in a second way, conceiving of that which is not real and conceiving of that which is real have the potential to be experiences of being in two really distinct ways. Each conception (of a golden mountain or of my golden ring) has with it both the being of a conception, but, according to Thomas (and verifiable in one's own experience), the potentiality to conform itself with extra-conceptual being. Each concept has within itself a potentiality of fulfillment in experience. This potentiality is what is referred to by the predicate "is true." This predicate does not add to being according to Aquinas. It expresses a mode of being common to all beings in a relational correspondence between the intellect, which has the conception, and the world which instantiates the properties of those conceived in the intellect. Thus, for both conceptions (of a golden mountain, or of the keys on my desk), each has the possibility of truth present within the conception. This possibility of truth remains a potentiality of the conception of the golden mountain, but an actuality of the conception of the keys on my desk when the conception is fulfilled by an act of experience of that which corresponds to it. This is only possible because the soul (following Thomas quoting Aristotle's *De Anima*) is "in some way all things."[2]

To assert the proposition, borrowed from Avicenna, which Aquinas begins his reply in Article 1 in the *Questions on Truth*, "that which the intellect first conceives as … the most evident … is being" is also to assert it to be true. Thus, necessarily to have an intellect which conceives is to have an intellectual awareness of the conception being true. Being true is a coextensive relational predicate necessarily present any time it is conceived. This is not too different from Descartes' *cogito*. Yet, here we are neither seeking a foundation for being, nor a foundation for certainty of all other being, nor our knowledge of it. I am simply arguing that if metaphysics, *that is, the study of being qua being*, is possible, then necessarily an account of truth is coextensive with it. If the first thing which the intellect conceives of is being, then necessarily, the intellect conceives of being containing the relational predicate "true." Thus, if the intellect conceives, it conceives of being first, and necessarily conceives of "being true." It follows that from being comes truth as the foundation for all intellectual life.

While the intellect first conceives being as that which is most evident, it is the reality of truth as a mode of being which allows the intellect to move from a mere conception of being to the real correspondence of one's conception of being to being outside of one's conception. When the intellect conceives of being (internal to the intellect), necessarily one conceives of one mode of being, namely, the predicate "is true." This predicate is a relational mode of being between the intellect itself and things (reality distinct from the intellect). Thus, when being is evident to the intellect, it points to truth as conformity of the intellect with things outside the intellect, and knowledge is produced as a result of this conformity.

Truth then, according to Aquinas, does not add to being. Rather "truth" is a real predicate which expresses a mode of being common to all beings in a relational correspondence. This, according to Thomas, "is possible only if there is something which is such that it agrees with every being." Such a being is the soul which "in some way is all things." Thus, the soul, being made in God's image, can potentially become all things. The soul, in an act of conceiving, conceives being first, and with being as such it also can see, with reflection, time and perhaps some hard work, that relational mode of being in which conceptual being in the intellect conforms with the being of things as such. Thus, metaphysics as the study of being logically carries truth with it, and with additional hard work, a full epistemology.

8.2 Metaphysics and correspondence

Following Aquinas, I have argued that ontology (metaphysics) entails an account of truth. I turn now to an argument with the conclusion that the only possible account of truth which can be logically coextensive with any possible metaphysics is a correspondence theory. At this point in my argument, I try to connect the idea that any propositional assertion contains within it the core of a correspondence view of truth which Aquinas (among others) advocated. The first step is to point out that propositions, whether they are present to the intellect in acts of assertion (acts of believing, claiming, denying, etc.) or can exist apart from those acts, carry with them *content* which is *about* something.[3] The property of intentionality had by propositions as such and propositions present in assertions by their very nature produce the potentiality for correspondence. For any proposition *p*, necessarily one property of *p* in virtue of it being *p* is to contain within itself what it is about. The very real nature of propositional intentionality is the potentiality for correspondence. Thus, all propositional assertions are things which contain the central aspects of one side of the correspondence relation in a correspondence theory of truth.

The next step in my argument is to show that all accounts of truth logically coextensive with any possible metaphysics are propositional assertions. This seems obvious. If any metaphysics is conceived, it is conceived by means of propositional content. Thus, whatever metaphysics one conceives, it will be generated my means of propositions which contain the central aspects of the correspondence theory of truth. Therefore, to do metaphysics, to have an ontology is to conceive of the way the world is. Conceiving and asserting the way the world is by means of intentional states (propositional or otherwise) just is to put forward the possibility of that metaphysics corresponding to the way the world is.

8.3 Realism

So far, I have tried to argue that metaphysics entails a theory of truth, and that any metaphysics of truth will be made by means of propositions which point to the possibility of truth as correspondence. The third stage of my argument is that the concept of truth as correspondence should be understood on a realistic account of universals. Since truth is a mode of being, I argue that only correspondence theories which are metaphysically robust can serve as the basis of the metaphysics of truth. If one is to develop an ontology, it must be done by recognizing that the concept of truth as correspondence which flows from the concept of being contains within it a conceptual requirement of realism about universals. In particular, I argue that only correspondence theories which rely upon a realistic understanding of universals (e.g., Platonism) can serve adequately as the basis of an epistemology of metaphysics.

There are several very recent possible candidates for a realistic correspondence account of truth. For example, consider William Alston's minimalism which makes use of the "T-schema"

(p) The proposition that *p* is true iff *p*.

There is, according to Alston, an "identity of content" between *p* on the left hand side of the bi-conditional and the right hand side. Alston never spells out what this identity consists in, although he indicates that this is the longer project of a full-blown correspondence theory of truth (Alston 1996, p. 33). Alston does assert that one's metaphysics is irrelevant to this minimal realism about truth (p. 78). He adds that his truth (alethic) minimalism is independent of one's views about the nature of universals as well. He states, "The nominalist about properties … can embrace alethic realism with as good a conscience as her realist rival" (p. 81). I believe Alston is very mistaken about this. Let us see why.

All correspondence views of truth rely upon a connection between that which is true (proposition, belief, statement, sentence, etc …) and that which makes true that which is true (reality, the world, facts, states of affairs, etc.). This connection, this correspondence must be one in which there are two things which have a relation which allows them to correspond. Nominalism as a metaphysical view cannot, in virtue of identifying properties with particulars or words, give the right kind of correspondence between the intellect and reality. For example, one could maintain that there is a kind of "exact" resemblance between the truth maker and the truth bearer, between the intellect and the world. Nominalists might rely on a metaphysical view of "abstract particulars" or tropes which exactly resemble one another. On a correspondence view of truth, the two relata in the correspondence relation would have to be particulars standing in an exactly resembling relation, where, for example, according to nominalist Keith Campbell, there is "no numerically identical item present in both" (Cambpell 1990, p. 31).

Here is where the trouble begins. Can the "exact resemblance" relation produce a correspondence between the thing and intellect such that the intellect really does conform to the way things are? The answer is no. The first problem is a purely logical one. Consider again Alston's T-schema: (p) The proposition that p is true iff p. According to the nominalist, "p" on the left side of the biconditional and "p" on the right side of the biconditional are not *the same* content. For, according to the nominalist metaphysics, there is nothing identical in both instances of "p." Thus, for any logical statement containing multiple instances of the same proposition (or any formalized argument for that matter), if a proposition is introduced (symbolically or otherwise), any further attempt to introduce the same proposition in either another simple statement or a complex proposition (e.g., *If p then, p if and only if q*) will literally not be an introduction of the same proposition. It will be a proposition which exactly resembles the first, but is literally not the same. Not only does this pose problems for simple arguments such as *modus ponens*: If p then q, p, therefore q, but also for a theory of truth. For if there is no straightforward identity among propositions expressed across logical inferences, then the conclusion of any instances of *modus ponens* will not be q, but rather $q*$ is not numerically identical to q but rather stands in an exactly resembling relation.[4] So, this indicates the first problem with nominalist metaphysics for a correspondence theory of truth.

A nominalist correspondence T-schema would be "(p) The proposition that p is true iff $p*$" where $p*$ would be something that "exactly resembles" p but in no way, contrary to Alston, has the same content as p. This might be another theory of truth, but it would in no way be a realist correspondence theory of truth, the type of which Alston claims to be offering. Even if it were put forward as another theory of truth, it would as argued above contain within it, in virtue of it being asserted by means of propositions, the potentiality of its own intentional fulfillment. By claiming that one's nominalism is true, one is relying upon (or perhaps presupposing) the idea that there *is* in fact a real identity between one's nominalist metaphysics and the way the world is, but nominalism can't handle such an identity! Thus, to assert nominalism is to assert that the theory is the way the world is, but this is to give up nominalism. One could qualify nominalism to tell us that there is an "exact resemblance" relation which stands between the way the world is and one's nominalist conceptions of the world. But this will not do.

The regress problem for nominalism enters here in at least two ways. First, it is possible to have multiple instances of the "exactly resembling" relation, but the question is, what makes both of these relations "exactly resembling"? Either "exactly resembling" becomes a universal which can be multiply instantiated (nominalism is given up) or an additional relation of "exactly resembling[1]" is introduced and an infinite regress looms large.[5] Second, it is possible for two intellects (minds) to conceive (believe, think, etc.) of the same proposition. Two people can believe that "2+2=4" or "London is north of Paris." If nominalism were true, no one is ever really thinking the same thing. Not only is this worrisome as a starting point for subjectivist relativism, it is also contrary to our ordinary experience of coming to see that people believe what we believe. At any rate, the regress problem still applies here, too. How the same proposition can be believed by multiple subjects will still require to appeal an "exact resemblance" relation functioning as a universal or requiring another "exact resemblance" relation to explain multiple instances of the exact resemblance relation among multiple minds instantiating the same belief. Thus, I conclude that nominalism cannot give us a real conformity of the intellect with things. By real conformity, I mean (following Aquinas) a conformity in which the intellect "is in some way" the thing it is conformed to.

What I have said in this section does not give us a full defense of realism about universals.[6] I intended this section to be a simple disjunctive syllogism (hopefully without committing a false dichotomy fallacy). Either nominalism or realism can best explain the identity of content between truth bearer and truth maker. It seems doubtful that nominalism can best explain the identity of content between truth bearer and truth maker. Therefore, realism can best explain the identity of content between truth bearer and truth maker.

Apart from this disjunctive syllogism there are at least two reasons why realism about universals can best explain the correspondence relation. Universals, realistically understood, allow for sameness across difference. The same universal can be present in multiple instances allowing for what Alston calls the "identity of content" between truth bearer and truth maker. This identity between truth bearer and truth maker is going to be much different than the identity that two red objects have, for example. For any two red objects, the universal redness will be fully present in each instance. For truth bearer and truth maker, the property of redness will really be *in* the instance of the particular thing, while for the truth bearer, redness will not be in the proposition (belief, sentence, etc.) in the same way redness is in the object. The proposition (using Aquinas' terms here, the conception of the intellect), will be *about* the instance of redness. This aboutness is of a particular instance of redness, but can only be of redness in virtue of its being *about* redness *qua* universal. Thus, the adequation of thing and intellect is fulfilled by means of the intellect's concept being about: (1) this red thing, (2) the red thing having being, and (3) the being in the concept and the being in reality both having their being in virtue of their relation to the universal redness. This is a brief sketch of how appeal to real universals can explain the correspondence relation. Suffice it to say that I believe that realism about universals can do the job better than nominalism.

8.4 Common sense

Finally, I believe that a correspondence theory based upon realism about universals is itself an instance of the ultimate nature of reality. We can experience this reality in our commonsense experiences. Everyone can know truth, because we are the kinds of beings who can find the world as we have thought it to be. Dallas Willard, elaborating Edmund Husserl's view of truth as adequation of thing and intellect (which I believe very closely follows Aquinas'), claims that whenever there is an act of the fulfillment of the intellect's conception by things, whenever there is a direct experience of the adequation of thing and intellect, a new thing arises in our experience. This new thing is an instance of being containing within it being as truth. The truth as adequation of thing and intellect appears to us, and our awareness of it "is directly experienced or lived through" (Willard 1984, pp. 228–229).

Truth can be instantiated in our common, ordinary lived experiences. When we see truth (especially in simple acts like finding my car keys where I believed them to be), we see an instance of being *qua* fulfillment of the adequation of intellect by things. This experience when examined gives us *knowledge* of truth. This realization, should we have our souls properly aligned (let's not forget that the soul is not exhausted by the intellect... the will is always with us), may lead us to further metaphysical inquiry. Why does truth have this objective structure? How do the intellect and things in the world maintain their own existence? Why is there truth at all?

The consequences of experiences of truth are twofold. First, these questions can entail truth in other areas of human inquiry. We will examine a few areas in the next chapter. Second, and more importantly, the lived experience of truth may stir in our hearts a restlessness that moves us to seek that ultimate source of truth. This is the life of a philosopher, a friend of wisdom who seeks and finds the truth because of a love of truth.

9

Truth Applied

9.0 Introduction

Throughout this introduction to truth, I have argued in favor of a view of truth as the adequation of thing and intellect. In this chapter, I consider how truth applies to three areas of human life: politics, economics, and religion. This chapter is a sample of my own reflections on the application of truth. In the first section, I argue that truth entails freedom as the basis for political life. In the second section, I argue that truth is crucial to a flourishing economic life. I also argue that a theory of truth applies to economic life not only at the individual level in virtues such as honesty and integrity, but also at a systemic level in areas such as trust and cooperation. In the last section, I consider whether religious claims can be true or false, or whether they are simply a matter of faith or belief.

9.1 Freedom

Truth is simple, and its simplicity entails freedom. Consider a simple example of an experience of truth. I reach for my keys in my backpack to unlock my car. They are not there. I believe that I have left my keys on my desk. I return to my office (the secretary lets me in for the third time this semester), and I look on my desk. I see my keys. I swipe them off the desk, mumble my apologies again to the secretary, call my wife to let her know I'll be late (again), and hurry to my car. Since I'm in a rush to get home, I'm not in a particularly philosophically reflective mood, but something extraordinary just occurred. This profound yet mundane event happens countless times for every human being capable of having everyday experiences. I knew truth. I experienced truth. This experience of truth exemplifies what truth essentially is: the fulfillment of a belief by things in the world, the adequation of thing and intellect.[1]

Truth as adequation of thing and intellect entails freedom in at least three senses. First, the adequation of thing and intellect entails rational freedom. When I experience truth, I am aware that within me lies the capacity to either accept the truth, or to reject it. This experience exemplifies before my mind the capacity for freedom in my will. Because I experience truth, I necessarily experience freedom. Thus, truth entails rational (intellectual) freedom.

Second, the adequation of thing and intellect entails moral freedom. When I believe that my keys are on my desk and I experience my keys being on my desk, I experience truth. I am aware that I can accept the truth or reject it. This awareness allows my will to manifest itself in action. I can act in accordance with truth or I can act contrary to the truth. This is fundamentally a moral choice. To act in accordance to what is real fulfills my nature as a rational being. If I choose to act contrary to the adequation of my intellect and the world, I profoundly reject my nature as a being which can know that its intellect is fulfilled. I act inconsistently with what I am. To do so continually and to the extreme is to become un-free, to become a slave.[2] Thus, the reality of my freedom when combined with a rejection of truth entails the enslavement of my will and the unmaking of my rational nature. Thus, truth entails moral freedom.

Third, the adequation of thing and intellect entails political freedom. My choice to act in accordance (or not) with the truth can have implications for others. I cannot relate socially as a human being, if acting according to a falsehood makes me un-human. My living a lie has consequences on others, violates the duties I have because of my relationships, and makes impossible the virtues required for those relationships to exist in the first place. Acting according to truth entails all possible social life, including political life. Thus, truth entails political freedom.

I have argued that truth entails freedom; let us turn to those truths which make us most free. Empirical truths, such as the matching of my belief that my keys are on my desk with the reality of my keys being on my desk, require us to experience the match between our beliefs and our perceptions in order to see that our beliefs are true. These truths give us some freedom. I am able to make it home for supper if I have my car keys! However, some truths do not require any empirical experience in order to see that they are true. Such truths are self-evident. There are no proofs for truths such as these. To form beliefs about them, to see them as they are in themselves, just is to see that they are true. Such truths are the foundation for all other truths. Unless some things are seen to be true without proof, nothing can be seen to be true by means of proof.[3] This foundational idea (or idea of foundationalism) entails the logical superiority of self-evident truths. Without them, no other truths could be had. Thus, among truths, self-evident truths are necessarily more foundational and logically superior to other truths.

Let us connect this idea of truth entailing freedom with the logical superiority of self-evident truths. This argument relies on the entailment relations between ideas or propositions of the same kind but which differ in their logical superiority *qua* foundationally necessary for other truths. Here is the framework for the inference.

1. If *p* entails *q*, and

2. *r* is logically superior than *p*, and

3. *r* is logically of the same kind as *p*, then

4. if *r* entails *s*, then

5. *s* is logically superior to *q* but of the same kind.

Applying this framework to the current discussion we have:

1. *Truths entails freedom, and

2. *Self-evident truths are logically superior truths, and

3. *Self-evident truths are truths, then

4. *Self-evident truths entail freedom*

5. *Freedom* is logically superior to freedom but of the same kind.

When the mind sees self-evident truths, it necessarily has the possibility of more freedom than when it sees ordinary empirical truths. The same applies then to morality and politics. If this reasoning works and if there are self-evident truths about reason, the will and politics, then seeing these truths entail the possibility of even greater freedom. Thus, examples of seeing self-evident moral truths make possible the actualization of great moral goodness.

Let us take an example. If we can see that certain political truths are self-evident, and we act on the freedom which we become aware of because of our awareness of such truths, then it is possible for us to actualize the truths we see self-evidently. Consider one such claim to self-evident truth:

> All men are created equal, that they are endowed by their Creator with certain unalienable Rights, that among these are Life, Liberty and the pursuit of Happiness.[4]

How do we come to see these truths? One of the primary difficulties (and perhaps one of the reasons that one might want to reject them altogether) about self-evident truths is that they are not the conclusions of arguments. They cannot be proved. Yet, how do we come to see them? I believe we come to see them by the same general means that we come to see simple truths in empirical experiences. How do I see the truth that my keys are on my desk? I go look. We look to see the truth of self-evident truths. The manner of looking is of course different than looking for our keys. It is quite impossible to see that $5 + 7 = 12$ by rummaging through one's office.[5]

How then do we look? Perhaps an analogy might help. I take basic color or sound experiences to be analogous to experiencing self-evident truths. In music, it is possible to "see" by hearing what the various notes are. In order to hear a C note, at least three things must occur.[6] First, one must be have one's ears functioning properly, not be wearing headphones, and not have other sounds drowning out the note. These are necessary pre-conditions for hearing a C note. Second, we also have to be willing to listen. If I refuse to listen to a C not played on a piano, by shouting "LALALALALALAL..." every time the note is played, I will never hear a C note. Third, there must be external conditions for the playing of the note; a piano or other instrument is needed to produce the note and make possible the conditions by means of which I experience it. One cannot hear a C note in a vacuum.

The analogy applies to self-evident truths about freedom itself. First, our heads, and indeed our hearts (to use the Platonic analogy), must be in the right place.[7] For if our minds are too dull or our will too corrupt, then we might not be able to see truths about freedom at all. Second, we must be willing to see these truths and act accordingly. Third, there may be external conditions needed to see such truths. Perhaps we need to look at what it means to be human in order to see that we have a right to life, in the same way we turn our ears in the direction of an instrument in order to hear a C note played. And of course it always helps to remember that the hearing of a C note or the seeing of a self-evident truth is not something that can be done for another person. It has to be done by oneself. Sometimes we must be trained to see such truths (only a virtuoso can notice certain tonal combinations), and sometimes we must be led so that we can see them for ourselves.

Now of course there are debates about whether or not a self-evident truth is a truth at all. These debates can take place in two different contexts. One context is with two interlocutors who both believe that self-evident truths are possible and knowable. Another context is with two interlocutors one of whom denies that self-evident truths are possible and knowable. It is only the former context in which real self-evident truths can be discovered. In the second context, no such progress is possible. Self-evident truths will become mere matters of personal preference or power. We accept the reasonableness of self-evident truths or we surrender to the animal in us.

We reach at last the ultimate limit of freedom. I have argued that truth entails freedom, self-evident truths entail greater freedom, awareness of self-evident truths about freedom entails more freedom, and knowledge of self-evident truths about freedom is possible but only under certain conditions. The conclusion is that an analysis of the simple awareness of truth in ordinary commonsense experience can serve as the basis for philosophical reflection on other areas of human life, including freedom. Our freedom, both in individual and political life, is grounded in truth. Without truth freedom is lost.

9.2 Economics

I argued in the previous section that truth entails freedom, and that self-evident truths entail greater freedom, and that self-evident truths about freedom entail even greater freedom. The experience of truth which entails freedom also brings with it self-knowledge. That is, when I experience the adequation of thing and intellect, I am aware that this adequation is possessed by me, that I am a self. Second, I recognize that I possess the adequation. It is mine. This self-knowledge entails not only that I possess my own thoughts, but that I possess my own self. I am a substance, a thing which has properties, but I am not had as a property by anything else. Thus, we have in our experience of truth an awareness of freedom and self-ownership. Third, I see that truth is independent of me. Although I can experience truth, the fundamental grounding of the adequation of thing and intellect is entirely dependent upon things distinct from me. Thus, I now stand in a relation of externality to the truths I experience. Finally, I find in my experiences, an awareness of truths which do not depend upon me. That a belief is true, for example, that my keys are on my desk, is independent of how I feel about things and independent from my beliefs and actions. I can believe all I want that my keys are in my backpack, or that they are in my car, or in my pocket, I can even jump up and downs screaming "My keys are in my pocket." But, if reality does not match my belief, no intensity of belief will change this fact.

Some beliefs, however, are dependent upon my actions for their being true (This discussion comes from Russell 1912). Some beliefs are made true by my beliefs which entail my acting in such a way as to make those beliefs true. For example, that I will be at Starbucks at 9:00 a.m. for coffee with some friends is made true by my belief that I will be at Starbucks at 9:00 a.m. *coupled with* my acting so as to *be* at Starbucks at 9:00 a.m. All of my actions by means of which I change the world around me appropriate into myself the world upon which I act. Our actions are the extensions of ourselves into the world. Thus, our actions can conform the world to be adequated to our intellects. Truth is adequation of thing and intellect. Our intellects form beliefs, our wills act to make the world conform to our beliefs and through this action, the world is made to be adequated to the intellect. I form a belief that a fallen tree can be created into a lovely piece of furniture, a chair, for example. I act by means of my will upon the basis of this belief in order to make of the fallen tree-trunk a piece of furniture.[8] My will entails action which conforms the world unto my belief. My will makes the world to be adequated to my intellect. This is still an adequation of thing and intellect. The belief that this tree trunk will be a made into a chair can only be adequated with reality by means of my action.

We see that an awareness of truth entails freedom and self-ownership. In addition, the engagement of the will to create things other than itself produces new truth which relate to the self by means of an extension of the self into the world. Truth entails freedom and self-ownership which when actualized manifest things other than the self but connected by freedom to the self. The soul extends itself into the world, and possesses it. This can be properly said to be the origins of property and ownership.[9] We move from truth to freedom, from freedom to the truth of the incorporation of things in the world to the self which is private property. As we can freely do or forbear with respect to ourselves, we can also do or forbear with respect to that which is an extension of the self that is with one's property. Thus, the reality of truth entails freedom and private property.

It is an obvious feature of human life that necessarily human beings are related to other human beings, and the most basic relationships are those of the family: mother, father, children upon which homes or households are founded. Properly speaking, economics is "oikos-nomos" or "rule of the home." The home is not only where the heart is, but it is also the beginning point of economic life. The home is the basic social reality constituted by the internal relations of its parts. The natural acts of conjugal relations between men and women which lead to the begetting of children occur in the context of human beings who not only belong to themselves, but act to possess things in the world around them. If combined with love, the reality of the family leads to the need to provide for the family those material goods without which human beings cannot live. Thus, from the love embodied in family, together with the real truth of freedom, economics (the rule of the household) becomes a reality.

The provision for one's household grounds itself in the extension of the self into the world which it inhabits. Food is collected, meat is hunted, fires are lit, and shelters are built. Those things which are essential to human life are drawn into the home by an exercise of the will in order to manifest the love which one has for one's family. The story is not terribly complex. Family begets family. Tribes form. Nations grow. The economy of the home *simpliciter* becomes more and more complex.

Let me summarize my two arguments thus far:

Argument 1:
P1.1 There is truth.
P1.2 If there is truth, then there is individual freedom.
P1.3 If there is individual freedom, then the soul can extend itself into the world.
P1.4 If the soul can extend itself into the world, then private property can be created.
P1.5 If private property can be created, then there is the possibility of free exchange of private property.
C1: Therefore, there is the possibility of free exchange of private property.

A necessary condition for the possibility of free exchange of private property is multiple individuals with private property. Thus, an additional argument is needed.

Argument 2:

P2.1 Necessarily, human beings are familial.

P2.2 If human beings are familial, then the needs of the family are to be provided for.

P2.3 If the needs of the family are to be provided for, then there is economics (the rule of the household).

C2: There is economics.

Thus, combining C1 and C2, we have both the reality of economics and the possibility of free exchange of private property. Given these two conclusions we come to both truths *about* economic life and the necessity of truth *in* economic life. Let us examine each of these in turn.

The truths *about* economic life which are intertwined with the arguments above have a fundamentally moral dimension. First, modes of economic life which undermine the family cannot be true. They make impossible the very thing which gives rise to economics. That is, any economic structure which undermines the family will make economics impossible. It is self-stultifying. Take for example this quotation from the *Communist Manifesto*: "Abolition of the family! Even the most radical flare up at this infamous proposal of the Communists…The bourgeois family will vanish as a matter of course when its complement vanishes, and both will vanish with the vanishing of capital" (Marx and Engels 1955, p. 27). Marxism with respect to economics cannot be true. It undermines the family which is the foundation of the ruling of the home. In addition, any system which undermines individual liberty cannot be a reasonable economic system for it too would stultify itself. While it may be possible for a wide range of economic systems to be consistent with our ordinary understanding of truth which entails individual freedom, any system of economics which undermines individual liberty or family structure as a precondition for economics as such will necessarily fail.

Truth, understood as the adequation of thing and intellect, is not only that by which economics arises, it is also a necessary condition for the continuation of economic activity. In addition to truths *about* economic life, truth must also exist *in* economic life in three ways. First, no economic act understood as an exchange of goods or services can exist without an adequation of thing and intellect. To propose an exchange of goods or services one must have a concept of the goods or services which are to be exchanged, and there must exist those things which are to be exchanged. Of course, the things which are to be exchanged can be ideas, but there must be both concept and object existing in both parties antecedent to the exchange. Truth is logically prior to economic activity.

Second, truth must exist for economic activity to be consummated. What is exchanged by the seller must be adequated to the intellect of the buyer. What is given in exchange for the thing sold must be adequated in the intellect of the seller. In other words, the commonsense notion of truth is always present in a fair economic exchange. It is when the adequation of thing and intellect is not present in an economic exchange that such an exchange can be considered unjust or unfair or unequal. Consider examples of receiving a defective product, receiving less of a product than one paid for or receiving a different product than was expected. In each of these cases, there is no adequation of thing and intellect on the part of the buyer. The buyer's intellect conceives of what is purchased (usually through representation presented on the part of the seller) and if that conception is not adequately fulfilled by the product purchased, then there is an interruption in the economic exchange. In extreme cases, there is outright fraud or theft.

Third, there is the need for an adequate representation of the way things are in the nature of interpersonal relationships in general and in economic life in particular. Without an adequation of thing and intellect, trust between and among rational agents becomes impossible. It is not because economic arrangements "work" or are pragmatically useful that we enter into them. Indeed, all macroeconomic arrangements which are functionally designed with pre-determined outcomes necessarily contain within them the possibility of running into a reality which was not foreseen. This entails a collapse of the pragmatic antecedent function into purely arbitrarily willed outcomes. Pragmatism at the economic level will suffer from the same problems as pragmatism at the level of truth. It is possible to have systems that fulfill someone's interest but are inconsistent with the way things are. Similarly, "coherence" of beliefs or economic activities can exist but not amount to a full realization of the capacities of the agents involved in an exchange. Economies restricted by severe state regulations might cohere internally, but they lack the full expression of the truly free abilities of those participating in them. Command economies violate freedom and truth grounded in individual experience.

The commonsense view of truth which each person experiences allows us to see truth exemplified in our ordinary experiences. Given the reality of our experiences of truth, we can see the connections between truth, liberty, and property. With this in mind, we can conceive of a view of economics which is grounded in human nature and act consistently with it. Seeing truth in ordinary ways allows us to conceive of truth in complex ways, including economics. Living according to truth in economic life may be a bit more complex than living according to truth when looking for one's car keys. Truth remains the same in both cases. Human flourishing in economic life requires understanding truth as the adequation of thing and intellect beginning with the individual and working outward to economic life.

9.3 Religion[10]

When teaching courses in religion and philosophy of religion (at both secular and religious institutions), I begin my classes by doing two things. First, I try to present reasons to think that relativistic thinking about truth is problematic. While there is a debate about whether professors ought to try to *convince* students that relativism is untenable intellectually (see Talbot 2012), students should at least be exposed to the problems with relativism. When it comes to religion, I put the question to my students by asking something like this, "Are there any right answers to religious questions?" Usually students respond with some sort of relativistic claims about religious beliefs and the truth of those beliefs being relative to the religions that maintain them.

Here are the problems with relativism in epistemology: it is self-defeating, rests on weak arguments, and is unlivable.[11] If the arguments against relativistic thinking are reasonable, then it is possible that there are truths regarding religious claims. I have argued in the previous chapters that truth is a matter of correspondence of mind to world which is seen in our commonsense experiences. Thus, if truth is possible in religion, then truth will be as simple as it is in ordinary experience: correspondence of thing and intellect.

The challenge for many is that while it is fairly obvious that religions make truth claims, those claims are often exclusivist vis-à-vis other religions. What are we to make of these exclusivist truth claims made by religions? We cannot retreat to relativism. Contradictory claims cannot both be true. Here are a few suggestions to consider.

First, one might begin by asking why a particular religion believes what they believe internal to their religion. Why do Hindus believe that cows are sacred? A discussion of the philosophical concept of *Brahman* could help make clear that Hindus believe that the divine permeates all things. Why do Muslims believe that the Koran should not be desecrated? A discussion of the nature of Islamic revelation might help here. Answering these questions cannot only help us see *that* religions make truth claims, but understand *why* they make such claims. Second, and more importantly than understanding *why* religions believe what they believe, we must think about what it means to come to discover whether a religious claim is true or not. This requires a clear understanding of what truth is. As I have argued throughout this book, I advocate starting with a commonsense concept of truth and working from there.

For example, if a student wants to know if it is true that there is ice cream being served in the cafeteria after school, they know intuitively how to find out if this is true. They simply go look. If reality matches their belief, then their belief is true. This is the commonsense view of truth as correspondence. A belief is true if it matches reality. Is my belief, "My keys are on my desk" true? I can find out by going to look for my keys on my desk. If the reality matches my belief, then my belief is true. I suggest to my students that finding out whether a religious claim is true or not is fundamentally no different in kind than going to look for one's keys. Of course, one does not look for God or heaven or nirvana in the same *way* as one looks for one's keys, but finding out whether or not a religious claim is true is still a matter of looking at the way things are (reality) and seeing if it matches up with one's beliefs. This will of course apply to religious disbelief as well. We can go and look at the world to see if religious claims are true or not. In a cultural environment where relativism is dominant, getting students to consider the possibility that religious claims could be true or false and encouraging them to consider whether they might be true or false can be both difficult but philosophically rewarding.

Once we have seen that the truth of religious claims is really possible, the problem of religious diversity does not go away. There are still very real and very opposing religious viewpoints that are common in public discourse. In what follows, I present a case for the real value of religious tolerance which rests upon both a rejection of relativism and a recognition of truth in general. In fact, a commitment to truth will be the foundational basis for a commitment to tolerance. If there were no truth to our religious beliefs, then tolerance as a virtue for public life would be impossible.

Let me begin with a claim that ought to be accepted by all reasonable people, regardless of religious belief (or lack thereof). Let us call this claim, the *principle of tolerance*.

> *The Principle of Tolerance*: The free exercise of religion should not be prohibited.

If you accept this principle, then you can't be a relativist about knowledge (or religion), and if you reject relativism (for the reasons given above), then you should accept this principle.

Here's the argument:

1. If the principle of tolerance is accepted as an objective moral reality, then one accepts the objectivity of truth.

2. If one accepts the objectivity of truth, then one must reject the idea that there is no truth in religion.

3. Therefore, if one is to maintain the principle of tolerance, then one must reject the idea that there is no truth in religion.

This inference is valid, but is it sound? The first premise is probably the controversial one. It could be false if one accepts the principle of tolerance, but does not accept it on the basis of the objectivity of truth. For example, the principle of tolerance could be a social construct. However, it would be difficult to argue for the principle of tolerance on anything other than purely pragmatic grounds. You could put the principle into practice on pragmatic grounds, but you can't rationally defend the principle, especially if *intolerance* were more pragmatically effective for your own goals. Attempting to believe in the principle of tolerance on pragmatic grounds puts you into the same kind of self-refuting problem we saw with pragmatism in Chapter 4. I might justify the principle of tolerance on socially pragmatic grounds, and you might justify *intolerance* on different socially pragmatic grounds. Thus, we have no rational grounds for defending our principles at all, and thus neither is reasonably established, including the idea that tolerance is better than intolerance. The conclusion is that if religious diversity is going to be tolerated in social life, then tolerance itself cannot be a value which is only pragmatically justified for a particular belief system. It must be a real objective value. It must be accepted by any reasonable person regardless of religious belief, including persons whose religious systems reject the social tolerance of religious diversity.

I've argued that rejecting relativism is necessary for the principle of tolerance, but is it sufficient? If we reject relativism, does this mean that we must accept the principle of tolerance? I believe that the answer is yes. Such an argument might run something like this:

1′. If one rejects religious relativism, then one accepts the objectivity of truth.

2′. If one accepts the objectivity of truth, then one must maintain the principle of tolerance.

3′. Therefore, if one rejects religious relativism, then one must maintain the principle of tolerance

1′ is true if relativism is rejected. The challenge here is 2′. It might be possible to accept the objectivity of truth, but reject the principle of tolerance as true. Does the truth of the principle of tolerance follow from the objectivity of truth itself? It might, if moral truths (of which the principle of tolerance is an instance) all "hang together"; if moral truths are logically internally related, such that the truth of one necessarily logically implies the other. If one accepts the truth of the objectivity of truth, then this necessarily implies the truth of the principle of tolerance.[12]

Rejecting 2' would require showing objectively that the principle of tolerance is false. One good reason to think that it is not false is that it derives its truth from human nature, especially the reality that human beings have free wills (as I have argued in Section 9.1) which can act, especially with respect to religious beliefs. Generally speaking, the defender of 2' should provide justification for the truth of the principle of tolerance from truths that are independent from any particular religious belief. This might require a more robust defense of something like the truth of natural moral law.

A more difficult case arises when a particular religious group maintains that one should reject the principle of tolerance on religious grounds. Doing so would be a clear rejection of 2'. Such a religious believer would maintain that freedom of epistemic practice requires a practical rejection of the principle of tolerance. The beliefs of the religion which are epistemically intolerant require the practice of intolerance and thus the general rejection of the truth of the principle of tolerance.

There are several ways to deal with a scenario like this. First, one could argue with the religious believer that they are mistaken about the truths of the commands of their religion. I suspect this would be unconvincing coming from an unbeliever in the religion in question. Second, one could argue for the reasonableness of the principle of tolerance on grounds which are rationally independent of the religion in question. This might work, if those grounds found some commonality to the beliefs held internal to the religion. More logically persuasive, one could point out that necessarily one religion's *practical* intolerance of the principle of tolerance would entail the impossibility of expressing religious beliefs altogether. In other words, denying the truth of the right to freely exercise one's religion would mean that one does not have the freedom to exercise one's religion in all cases, including the case of wanting to exercise one's religion with respect to doing away with the principle of tolerance. It appears viciously circular to reject the principle of tolerance on such religious grounds.

I have argued that if you maintain the principle of tolerance, then relativism about truth must be rejected, and the truth of the principle of tolerance flows from this rejection. This truth, accepting the principle of tolerance from a rejection of relativism, applies to everyone regardless of religious commitment or lack thereof. One could be a religious skeptic or an atheist and maintain that the principle of tolerance is a good thing. In addition, even if adherents to different religions maintain very different views of the nature of reality, or have views which are intolerant of other religions, it is possible to see, as result of the kind of rational reflection presented here, that the principle of tolerance is a good thing. The argument presented here is made independent of any religious belief.[13] The truth of the principle of tolerance is a real value and provides the context for understanding, studying, and evaluating the truth of religious beliefs. These truth claims will either match or not match the reality which they are about. Our job as philosophers is to seek and find the truth.

9.4 Conclusion

I have argued throughout this book that truth is simple. Truth can be found in our ordinary experiences. In this chapter, I have argued that it is from our ordinary experiences that we can have extended knowledge of truth in other areas of human life, including political freedom, economics, and religion. I believe the same will apply to all areas of human inquiry including science, the arts, morality, literature, and auto-mechanics. It will always be possible to see the truth in the match of our intellects with the world. This simplicity of truth and our understanding of it is what sets us free as human beings, not only in our love of wisdom, but in the things we do with our knowledge of truth. If truth in the ordinary common acts of finding the world as we thought it would be is the beginning of our love of truth, then what is the end? The ultimate end of truth would be the fullness of our intellect matching the fullness of reality. This seems impossible for finite minds, and indeed may give us something to do for eternity as immortal souls. Yet, in the meantime, if truth were fully revealed in commonsense reality, the fullness of truth embodied in a personal form, our knowledge of it might serve as the starting point of the fullness of a mind fully conformed to reality both now and forever.

Notes

Chapter 1

1   C.S. Peirce writes, "Ideoscopy consists in describing and classifying the ideas that belong to ordinary experience or that naturally arise in connection with ordinary life, without regard to their being valid or invalid or to their psychology" (Peirce 1904, p. 328).

2   See Aristotle (1984), *Metaphysics* 1047a, pp. 20–30.

3   For a good starting point to study perception, and a defense of the view assumed in this book, see Chapter 1 of Audi (2010).

4   I owe all of my insights into this section, and nearly all of my thinking about truth in a commonsense way to Dallas Willard. See especially Willard (1991).

5   These ideas are adapted from C.S. Lewis' book, *The Four Loves* (Lewis 1960).

6   See St. Paul's Letter to the Corinthian Church, Chapter 13 verses 4–6 (Holy Bible 1993).

7   See Willard (1999) for some practical points on this matter.

Chapter 2

1   Norman Kretzmann indicates that for Aquinas, truth is the appropriated attribute of the son, and "as an appropriated attribute [it clarifies] the relationship between the first and second persons [of the Trinity]; and ... it develops a metaphorically proper attribution of truth that is worth considering as an understanding of Jesus' claim to be the truth" (Kretzmann 1989, p. 99).

2   *De vera religione*, XXXVI, cited in Aquinas on Truth, p. 6.

3   See his *Metaphysical Disputations*, 8, Section 7, Par 25 (Suarez 1960, p 145).

4   Aquinas (1952, p 7).

5   See Hume (1978) Book III "Of Morals," Part I "Of Virtue and Vice in General."

Chapter 3

1   James O. Young (2008) gives an excellent overview of the two main objections to coherence theories of truth. The first is what Young calls the Specification Objection: We can have two contradictory sets of coherent beliefs, but cannot specify which is true and which is false. Young indicates that this objection comes from Betrand Russell (1907). Second, there is the "Transcendence Objection" which is the idea that a belief can be true without coherence. The belief about my keys being in an MIT lab was meant to be a belief of this sort: true, but incoherent with my system of beliefs.

2   I owe this insight to Dallas Willard.

3   He states, "Truth consists in" the "systematic coherence" of judgments (p. 27). See also p. 29 in his discussion of how a coherence doctrine falls short of being truth, as truth itself only pertains to the whole of what is real.

4   Indeed it is difficult to see how his view does not lead to solipsism either. Each person lives in their own little world, and my world constructs your world!

5   "The solid piers of fact, supposed to be standing there in broad daylight as the bases of our structure of theory, are illusion. There are no such things. The 'facts' that were to support our system are themselves relative to the system. In short, the coherence of judgments within a system is our test, and our only test, of any truth or fact whatever" (Blanshard, p. 215).

6   " 'Take the judgment,' That bird is a cardinal. If you heard someone make that remark, how would you test it? You would look and see. If there was a correspondence between what was asserted and what you saw, you would call the judgment true; if not, false. This is the way we actually assure ourselves of the truth of all such judgments, and it is correspondence that assures us" (p. 228). Blanshard responds,

> Now, plausible as this argument is, it goes to pieces on inspection. It assumes that, corresponding to our judgments, there is some solid chunk of fact, directly presented to sense and beyond all question, to which thought must adjust itself. And this "solid fact" is a fiction. What the theory takes a s fact and actually uses as such is another judgment or set of judgments, and what provides the verification is the coherence between the initial judgment and these. (p. 228)

7   An adverbial view developed along the lines of Robert Audi
     might also militate against Blanshard's skepticism toward
     correspondence theories here. Also in Chapter 8, I will argue
     that a realist defense of universals which will allow for a direct
     connection between truth bearer (the intellect) and truth maker
     (things) can also be used to develop a "naive" direct realist
     account of perception.

8   This will have to include such facts as: "7+5 = 12", "All vixens
     are female", "London is north of Madrid", "Yellow is brighter than
     brown." One should begin to wonder here how beliefs, coherent
     or incoherent, could determine any of these facts.

9   These ideas were presented by Dallas Willard in lectures on the
     Ontology of Knowledge at Biola University in the summer of 1997.
     See also Mosteller (2006) for my critique of a "No Common World,
     Therefore Relativism" argument presented by Chris Swoyer (1982)
     and see Mosteller (2008) chapter "Ontological Relativism" for a
     critique of similar ideas in the philosophy of William James and
     Hilary Putnam.

Chapter 4

1   I owe my ideas in this chapter of C. S. Peirce and William James
     to Susan Haack. The ideas presented in this chapter come from
     my notes from her lectures at the University of Miami. Professor
     Haack opened my interest to both early and recent pragmatism.
     Any errors in this chapter or misunderstandings of Peirce or James
     are entirely my own.

2   See Peirce's "How to Make Our Ideas Clear" (Thayer 1982).

3   This section is directly adapted from Yong and Haack (2010).

4   See Mosteller (2006) on Richard Rorty's relativistic tendencies.

5   It is important to note that Peirce puts this determination of
     habit in the subjunctive when he states that the identity of a
     habit depends on how it "**might** lead us to act ... under such
     circumstances as **might** possibly occur" (p. 87) [emphasis added].
     Peirce's ultimate formulation of the pragmatic maxim will be given
     in subjunctive form.

6   The bracketed numbers are to indicate the three types of
     experiences to which Peirce appeals as he develops his
     formulation of the pragmatic maxim.

7   See Houser (1999, p. xxiv) for a brief discussion of this concept in
     Peirce.

8   This paragraph is directly adapted and summarized from Haack (2004).

9   As with Peirce, I owe my understanding and criticisms of James' view of truth to ideas presented by Susan Haack.

10   Other pragmatists during the time of James and Peirce held similar views. Like James, Josiah Royce (1855–1916) held that truth was a form of correspondence in a loose, subjective sense when he states, "But what then is the test of the truthful correspondence of an ideal to its object, if object and idea can differ so widely? The only answer is in terms of Purpose. The idea is true if it possesses the sort of correspondence to its object that the idea itself wants to possess" (Royce 1959, p. 306). John Dewey (1859–1952) continues this sort of pragmatic version of the correspondence theory by parsing the word "correspondence" to mean "co" + "respondence." The world and thought respond together in a certain way. However, this need not mean the identity of thought and object, rather the "working" of object due to human thought. In his "The Practical Character of Reality" Dewey states, "For ordinary purposes, that is for practical purposes, the truth and the realness of things are synonymous." However, Dewey's view is that reality is only good, and thus true, when it conforms to the values set on it by human beings. He states, "Since it is a certain *kind* of object which we want, one which will be as favorable as possible to a consistent and liberal or growing functioning, it is this kind the *true* kind, which for us monopolizes the title of reality. Pragmatically, teleologically, this identification of truth and 'reality' is sound and reasonable" (Thayer, p. 284).

11   It is important to see the rhetoric of this passage which belies a false dichotomy. James seems to presuppose that we either have "vague statements" from "slouchy epistemologists" who just talk about correspondence without further analysis of the correspondence relation, or we have a real "concrete" satisfactory account which involves successful leading to reality. James gives no good reason to think that a correspondence view cannot give a successful account of what correspondence amounts to.

12   I owe this insight to Susan Haack.

13   See James' ideas about the spilled beans in James (1926). I argue that this is a form of highly problematic *ontological* relativism which is also taken up by Hilary Putnam (Mosteller 2008).

14   In the ideas in the sections here on Peirce and James, both the exposition and criticisms are derived from the works of Susan Haack.

15 I am of course assuming here that moral truths are as objective as truths about where my car keys are located.

16 I am grateful to the insights and criticism of my ideas in this section which were given to me by María José Frápolli and other members of the philosophy department at the University of Granada where I presented an early version of this portion of the book. If there are errors in my understanding of Brandom's projects, or weaknesses in my criticisms, they are entirely my own.

17 An anaphora is a word (or sentence) that refers back to a previous word; from the Greek "carry back."

18 "The prosentential approach to truth-talk not only supports the claim that the use of 'true' presupposes a notion of *semantic content*, and so cannot be the basis of an *explanation* of that notion, but also shows how to build an account of truth-talk out of an account of semantic content. Since we now have in view the possibility of explaining semantic content in terms of role in reasoning, we have in place the raw materials the prosentential theory needs to elaborate the important *expressive* (not explanatory) role that 'true' plays" (Brandom 2009, p. 173).

19 For an excellent summary of the background, history, presentation, and various lines of criticism and countercriticism to this argument, see Cole (2009), "The Chinese Room Argument."

20 For an approach to truth in a similar vein as Brandom's, see Frápolli (2012). In this work Frapoli states, "One does not know the meaning of truth without understanding the combinatorial task performed by the truth predicate and the rest of truth-words as they occur in different phrases" (Frápolli 2012, p. 22). I would argue that it is just the other way around. Even if one does exhaustively know the way in which truth is used linguistically, one would lack knowledge of the meaning of truth.

21 One concern with this objection is that it is unfair to assume that there could be other language games that we play. One could claim that for human beings there is only one language game going, and it is the one we all play as human beings. To say that we could construct another language game (where affirming the consequent could be part of the game) is just disingenuous. However, it still seems (at least) logically possible to construct another language game and attempt to live by it. In fact, it doesn't seem impossible to conceive that affirming the consequent could turn out to contribute greatly to our survival. Suppose it were evolutionarily advantageous to constantly affirm the consequent. Suppose this contributed to a language game which contains

the practice of granting an entitlement to believe arguments containing instances of affirming the consequent. Our world could have turned out this way, even if it did not. This possibility is meant to show that the reducibility of the normativity of truth to social practices is problematic.

Chapter 5

1   While there are various approaches to identity and difference in universals and particulars, I will argue in Chapter 8 that realism about universals/properties is the best way to understand universals in light of our experiences of truth.

2   I argued in Chapter 1 that forming a belief cannot be linguistic … so there's nothing linguistic going on here at all.

3   For example, on Thomas Aquinas' view of truth, the soul can agree or in Frege's language "correspond perfectly" with all things. Aquinas quotes Aristotle when he says the soul in some way "is all things" (Aquinas 1952). Patrick Lee put's the relation this way, "While there is identity of form or content, the mode of being of the form in the thing is different from its mode of being in the intellect's act" (Lee 1986, p. 58).

4   This is reminiscent of Roderick Chisholm's *The Problem of the Criterion* (Chisholm 1973).

5   This is not to say that a "thought" in Frege's sense (or a proposition) is not true independent from acts of judging. It is because a thought is true, even if no human being has ever had it, that we can judge it to be true.

6   This is rather unfortunate for many great thinkers in the history of philosophy.

Chapter 6

1   This survey is not exhaustive. One omission is G. E. Moore. Twentieth-century commentators are divided as to whether or not G. E. Moore held to the correspondence theory. See Schmitt (1995) for a defense of Moore's support of correspondence. See Fredrick Copleston who maintains that Moore rejects the correspondence theory in an article on the nature of judgment published in *Mind* in 1899 (Copleston 1995, vol. VIII, p. 403).

2   "Sentence" or "statement" might be included along with
     propositions. The former two items may be ontologically
     dependent on the latter.

3   This example is presented by Susan Haack in (2004), p. 428.

4   This also might be the case because there is no objective "world"
     with which one's mind can be related. This objection to truth as
     correspondence was considered in the chapter on coherentism.

5   There are also puzzles about truth of things, states of affairs, etc.,
     that will exist in the future. Puzzles about future truths may also be
     a reason to reject any view of correspondence which requires the
     present existence of things as one of the items in the relation.

6   Facts seem to be ontologically dependent on things for their
     coming into being, but not for the continuance of their being.
     When a thing exists, a fact which is of that thing also exists. When
     a thing quits existing, facts about that thing continues to exist,
     including facts about the things' temporal properties.

7   The numbers following quotations refer to Wittgenstein's divisions
     of the *Tractatus*. *Tractatus Logico-Philosophicus* in Wittgenstein
     (1961).

8   The sense to which Wittgenstein refers here is what a picture,
     thought, and now proposition represent, namely a possible state
     of affairs.

9   Sections 5.5, 5.6 in this chapter and 6.2 in the following chapter
     first appeared in Mosteller (2010).

10   See Russell (1959), pp. 181–182.

11   I will consider Edmund Husserl's view of this point in the following
     chapter.

Chapter 7

1   For a defense of this position, see Moreland (1989).

2   Special care must be given to propositions that are about non-
     existent objects, or propositions that are paradoxical (e.g., the
     strengthened liar paradox). Husserl considers such propositions in
     his 1898 article "Intentional Objects" (Husserl 1994). It seems that
     there may just be more propositions that exist as universals than
     there are real objects that correspond to them. All propositions can
     be instanced as objects of thought, but not all intentional contents
     of propositions are instanced in real objects.

3   This can be applied directly to the versions of coherence and
     pragmatism which were addressed in previous chapters on those
     topics.

4   I understand Husserl to mean by Idea, and Species the same
     things as Platonic form or universal. I will use these terms
     interchangeably in my description of the passages that are being
     examined.

5   While Husserl uses the Thomistic language of "adequation of thing
     and intellect" it is not clear to me how the two might differ on
     the relation of truth and the existence of minds. Aquinas explicitly
     says that truth as a relation (or relational property) would not exist
     without minds (if it were possible for God's mind not to exist).
     On could put such Ideas which Husserl considers here in the
     mind of God in order to have a consistent view between Husserl
     and Aquinas. Husserl simply does not address here the issue of
     a divine mind and the connection of truth in this portion of the
     Logical Investigations.

6   This might be the makings of a critique of deflationism; p and "p is
     true" *qua* judgment are distinct.

7   Whether we need a divine mind or other minds at all is not of
     course disputed by other correspondence theorists such as
     Aquinas.

8   The ontological status of such logical "laws" might be questioned
     here. It might be possible, along Thomistic lines, to account for
     such by appeal to a divine mind. One might ask whether there is a
     need to further ground the existence of such logical laws. Husserl
     appears to accept their existence without explanation. Plato or
     Aristotle might explain their being in light of a greater being (e.g.,
     the Form of the Good, a "demiurge" or a Prima Mover).

9   Both coherentist idealism (Alcoff) and pragmatic linguisticism
     (Brandom) maintain (in different ways) the immanence of truth in
     coherence of beliefs or social practices. Neither seem to allow for
     the transcendence of truth as does Husserl's realism.

10   This may require a defense of a direct realist view of perception.
     See Audi (2003) Chapter 1.

11   I derived this analogy from Dallas Willard in Willard (1991). Indeed,
     this whole chapter and much of this book is indebted to Willard's
     ideas in that work.

12   See 7.2 for a brief explanation of this point as a possible defeater
     for Husserl's view.

13   This section originally appeared in Mosteller (2010).

Chapter 8

1   I use the terms "metaphysics" and "ontology" interchangeably.

2   This generalization of the comprehension of truth as a mode of being from reflection on being *qua* being may give us a necessary condition for any correspondence theory of truth: it will require an account of the soul which has the faculty of reason which has the capacity to become all things. It seems dubious to me that such a capacity could be had on a naturalist/materialist account of the mind or soul.

3   I am assuming quite a lot about propositions here and the work they will be doing in this account of truth. Perhaps it is possible that even if propositions are not that which the intellect uses to make assertions, whatever is used by the intellect to make assertions contains within itself an intentionality, an "aboutness" which points to the possibility of correspondence. I believe a specific argument to the conclusion that propositions are the best candidate for intellectual assertion may be needed here.

4   I want to avoid creating a straw man here. I simply raise these difficulties here to point out the types of problems for a correspondence view of truth that a nominalist will face. A longer rejoinder to possible nominalistic objections to my criticisms of nominalism is certainly required for a robust defense of the view I am presenting here.

5   See Moreland (2001) for a lengthy discussion of both varieties of nominalism and their concomitant problems.

6   See Moreland (2001) for such a defense.

Chapter 9

1   Thomas Aquinas, *Questions on Truth*, Question 1, Article 1; and Edmund Husserl, *Logical Investigations*, Investigation VI, Chapter 5.

2   Lady Philosophy tells Boethius: "I know another cause of thy disease, one, too, of grave moment. Thou hast ceased to know thy own nature" in *Consolation of Philosophy* book VI.

3   C. S. Lewis, *Abolition of Man*, Chapter 2 "The Way."

4   U.S. *Declaration of Independence*.

5   As Robert Audi states in *Epistemology: A Contemporary Introduction to the Theory of Knowledge*, 3rd. ed. (Routledge, 2010), p. 118,

> Moreover, regardless of what produces our arithmetic beliefs initially, when they are justified in the way my belief that $7 + 5 = 12$ now is, experience does not appear to be what justifies them. For my part, I do not see precisely how the truth of the proposition might be grounded in the behavior of objects when they are combined; and I would not try to justify it, as opposed to illustrating it, by citing such behavior. (Audi 2003, p. 118)

6   Lewis, *Abolition of Man.*, Chapter 1 "Men Without Chests."

7   *Republic*, Book IV.

8   See Pieper (2011) for an excellent discussion of the relationship between truths that are independent and dependent on the mind.

9   These ideas are best presented by John Locke in his *Second Treatise of Civil Government* (Locke 1996).

10   This portion of the chapter originally appeared in in a longer paper in Mosteller (2013).

11   See Mosteller (2007) for a longer critique of relativism in philosophy generally.

12   For a fascinating and rigorous defense of this view applied to education, see Lewis (1974).

13   Special thanks to Andrew Fiala for emphasizing this point.

Works Cited

Alcoff, Linda. 2001. "A Case for Coherence" in *The Nature of Truth*. Edited by Michael Lynch. Cambridge, MA: MIT Press.

———. 2008. *Real Knowing*. Ithaca, NY: Cornell University Press.

Alston, William. 1996. *A Realist Conception of Truth*. Ithaca, NY: Cornell University Press.

Anselm. 1967. "De Veritate" in *Truth, Freedom and Evil: Three Philosophical Dialogues*. Edited and translated by Jasper Hopkins and Herbert Richardson. New York: Harper and Row.

Aquinas, Thomas. 1952. *Disputed Questions on Truth*. Translated by Robert W. Mulligan. Chicago: Regnery, http://dhspriory.org/thomas/QDdeVer1.htm#1.d

Aristotle. 1984. "'Metaphysics.'" in *The Complete Works of Aristotle, Volume II*. Edited by Jonathan Barnes. Translated by W.D. Ross. Princeton, NJ: Princeton University Press.

Audi, Robert. 2003. *A Contemporary Introduction to the Theory of Knowledge*, 3rd. Edition. New York: Routledge.

Augustine. 1910. *The Soliloquies of St. Augustine*, Translated by Rose Elizabeth Cleveland. Boston: Littleton Brown and Co.

Austin, J.L. 1979. "Truth" in *Philosophical Papers*, 3rd Edition. Edited by J.O. Urmson and G.J. Warnock. Oxford: Oxford University Press.

Blanshard, Brand. 1939. *The Nature of Thought, Vol. 2*. London: Gorge Allen & Unwin.

Boethius. 1999. *Consolation of Philosophy*. London: Penguin Books.

Bolzano, Bernard. 1972. *Theory of Science*, Edited and translated by Rolf George. Los Angeles: University of California Press.

Bosanquet, Bernard. 1911. *Truth and Coherence*. Glasgow: Robert Maclehose and Co. Ltd.

Bradley, F.H. 1914. *Essays on Truth and Reality*. Oxford: Clarendon Press.

Brandom, Robert. 1988. "Pragmatism, Phenomenalism and Truth Talk" in *Midwest Studies in Philosophy, Volume XII: Realism and Antirealism*. Edited by, Peter A. French, Theodore E. Uehling Jr., and Howard K. Wettstein. Minneapolis: University of Minnesota Press.

———. 1994. *Making it Explicit*. Cambridge, MA: Harvard University Press.

———. 2008. "Towards and Analytic Pragmatism" *Philosophical Topics*, Vol. 36, No. 2, pp. 1–27.

———. 2009. *Reason in Philosophy*. Cambridge, MA: Harvard
   University Press.
Campbell, Keith. 1990. *Abstract Particulars*. Oxford: Blackwell, 1990.
Chisholm, Roderick. 1973. *The Problem of the Criterion*. Marquette, WI:
   Marquette University Press.
Cole, David. "The Chinese Room Argument" *The Stanford Encyclopedia
   of Philosophy*, http://plato.stanford.edu/entries/chinese-room/.
Copleston, Frederick. 1993. *History of Philosophy*. New York: Image.
correspondence. 1990. *Webster's Ninth New Collegiate Dictionary*.
   Springfield, MA: Merriam Webster.
Dauer, Francis W. 1974. "In Defense of the Coherence Theory of Truth"
   The Journal of Philosophy, Vol. 71, No. 21, pp. 791–811.
Descartes, Renee. 1988. "*Discourse on Method*" in *Descartes Selected
   Philosophical Writings*, Translated by John Cottinham, Robert
   Stoothoff, and Dugald Murdoch. Cambridge: Cambridge University
   Press.
Frápolli, María José. 2012. *The Nature of Truth*. Dordrecht: Springer.
Frege, Gottlob. 1956. "The Thought: A Logical Inquiry" *Mind*, Vol. LXV,
   No. 259, pp. 289–311.
Fumerton, Richard. 1994. "The Incoherence of Coherence Theories"
   Journal of Philosophical Research, Vol. XIX, pp. 89–102.
———. 2002. *Realism and the Correspondence Theory of Truth*.
   Lanham, MD: Rowan and Littlefield.
Haack, Susan. 2004. "Realism." in *Handbook of Epistemology*. Edited
   by Ilkka Niiniluoto and Matti Sintonen. Dordrecht, The Netherlands:
   Kluwer.
———. 2006. "Pragmatism Old and New." in *Pragmatism Old and New*.
   Edited by Susan Haack and Robert Lane . New York: Prometheus.
Hegel, G.W.F. 1949. *The Phenomenology of Mind*, Translated by J.B.
   Baillie. London: Allen Unwin.
Hesiod. 1991. *Works and Days*. Edited by Richmond Lattimore. Ann
   Arbor, Michigan: Michigan University Press.
Holy Bible. 1993. New York: Harper Torch.
Homer. 1919. *The Oddysey*, Translated by A.T. Murray. Cambridge, MA:
   Harvard University Press.
———. 1924. *The Illiad*, Translated by A.T. Murray. Cambridge, MA:
   Harvard University Press.
Horwich, Paul. 2000. *Truth*, 2nd Edition. Oxford: Blackwell.
———. 2008. "Being and Truth" in *Midwest Studies in Philosophy: Truth
   and Its Deformities*. Edited by Peter French and Howard Wettstein.
   Oxford: Wiley-Blackwell.
Houser, Nathan. 1992. "Introduction" in *The Essential Peirce*. Edited by
   Nathan Houser and Christian Kloesel. Indianapolis: Indiana University
   Press.

Hume, David. 1978. *A Treatise of Human Nature*, Edited by L.A. Selby-Bige. Oxford: Clarendon Press, 1978.

Hurley, Patrick. 2012. *A Concise Introduction to Logic*, 11th edition. New York: Wadsworth.

Husserl, Edmund. 1970. *Logical Investigations*, Translated by J.N. Findlay. London: Routledge and Kegan Paul.

———. 1994. *Early Writings in the Philosophy of Logic and Mathematics*, Translated by Dallas Willard. Boston: Kluwer.

Jackson, Frank. 1982. "Epiphenomenal Qualia" *Philosophical Quarterly*, Vol. 32, pp. 127–136.

———. 1986. "What Mary Didn't Know" *Journal of Philosophy*, Vol. 83, pp. 291–295.

James, William. 1909. *The Meaning of Truth*. New York: Longmans, Green and Co.

———. 1926. "Letter to Dickinson S. Miller dated August 5, 1907" in *The Letters of William James, Volume 2*. Edited by Henry James. Boston: Little, Brown.

———. 1968. "Pragmatist Account of Truth" in *The Meaning of Truth*. New York: Greenwood.

Kant, Immanuel. 1929. *Critique of Pure Reason*, Translated by Norman Kemp Smith. New York: St. Martin's Press.

Kirk, G.S., Raven, J.E and Schofield, M. 1984. *The Presocratic Philosophers*. Cambridge: Cambridge University Press.

Klein, Peter and Warfield, Ted A. 1994. "What Price Coherence?" *Analysis*, Vol. 54, No. 3, pp. 129–132.

Kretzmann, Norman. 1989. "Trinity and Transcendentals" in *Trinity, Incarnation and Atonement*. Edited by Ronald J. Feenstra and Cornelius Plantinga Jr. Notre Dame: Notre Dame University Press.

Lee, Patrick. 1986. "Aquinas on Knowledge of Truth and Existence" *The New Scholasticism*, Vol. 60, No. 1, pp. 46–71.

Lewis, C.S. 1960. *The Four Loves*. New York: Harcourt Brace.

———. 1974. *The Abolition of Man*. New York: Harper Collins.

Locke, John. 1975. *An Essay Concerning Human Understanding*, Edited by Peter H. Nidditch. Oxford: Clarendon Press.

———. 1996. *Locke: Two Treatises of Government*, Edited by Peter Laslett. Cambridge: Cambridge University Press.

Macdonald, George. 1999. *Unspoken Sermons I, II, III*. Whitehorn, California: Johannesen.

Marx, Karl and Engels, Friedrich. 1955. *Communist Manifesto*. New York: Appleton-Centry-Crofts.

Milgram, Elijah. 2000. "Coherence: The Price of the Ticket" *The Journal of Philosophy*, Vol. 97, No. 2, pp. 82–93.

Moreland, J.P. 1989. "Was Husserl a Nominalist?" *Philosophy and Phenomenological Research*, Vol. XLIX, No. 4, pp. 661–674.

———. 2001. *Universals*. Montreal: McGill-Queen's University Press.

Mosteller, Timothy. 2006. *Relativism in Contemporary American Philosophy*. London: Continuum.

———. 2008. *Relativism: A Guide for the Perplexed*. London: Continuum.

———. 2010. "Platonism and Recent Correspondence Theories of Truth" *Southwest Philosophy Review*, Vol. 26, No. 1, pp. 197–204.

———. 2013. "Religious Diversity, Tolerance and Truth" in *Civility, Religious Pluralism and Education*. Edited by Vincent Biondi and Andrew Fiala. New York: Routledge.

Newman, Andrew. 2002. *The Correspondence Theory of Truth*. Cambridge: Cambridge University Press.

Olshewsky, Thomas M. 1983. "Peirce's Pragmatic Maxim" *Transactions of the Charles S. Peirce Society*, Vol. XIX, No. 2, pp. 199–210.

Olsson, Erik, 2012. "Coherentist Theories of Epistemic Justification," *The Stanford Encyclopedia of Philosophy*, Winter 2012, Edited by Edward N. Zalta, http://plato.stanford.edu/archives/win2012/entries/justep-coherence/.

Parmenides. 1964. *Truth*. in *Presocratic Philosophers*, edited by Geoffrey S. Kirk, and John E. Raven. Cambridge: Cambridge University Press.

Peirce, C.S. 1904. "A Letter to Lady Welby" in *Collected Papers of Charles Sanders Peirce*, Vol. 8. Edited by Arthur W. Burks. Cambridge, MA: Harvard University Press.

———. 1935. "Pragmatism: The Normative Sciences" in *The Collected Papers of Charles Sanders Peirce*. Edited by Charles Hartshorne and Paul Weiss. Cambridge, MA: Harvard University Press..

Pieper, Josef. 2011. *Living the Truth*. San Francisco: Ignatius Press.

Plato. 1871. "Republic" Translated by Benjamin Jowett, http://classics.mit.edu/Plato/republic.mb.txt

———. 1891. "Apology" Translated by Benjamin Jowett, http://classics.mit.edu/Plato/apology.html

———. 1997a. "Sophist." Translated by Nicholas P. White in *Plato Complete Works*. Edited by John M. Cooper. Indianapolis, Indiana: Hackett.

———. 1997b. "Theatetus" Translated by Myles Burnyeat in *Plato Complete Works*. Edited by John M. Cooper. Indianapolis, Indiana: Hackett.

Royce, Josiah. 1959. *The World and the Individual*, Vol. 1. New York: Dover Publications.

Rummel, R.J. 1997. *Death by Government*. Piscataway, NJ: Transaction.

Russell, Bertrand. 1907. "On the Nature of Truth" *Proceedings of the Aristotelian Society*, Vol. 7, pp. 228–249.

———. 1910. *Philosophical Essays*. London: Longmans.

———. 1912. *The Problems of Philosophy*. New York: Holt and Company.

———. 1919. "On Propositions: What They are and How They Mean" *Logic and Knowledge*. Edited by Robert Charles Marsh. New York: Routledge, pp. 283–321.

———. 1927. *Philosophy* (Published in Britain as *Outline of Philosophy*). New York: W.W. Norton.

———. 1940. *Inquiry into Meaning and Truth*. New York: W.W. Norton.

———. 1948. *Human Knowledge: Its Scope and Limits*. London: George Allen & Unwin.

———. 1959. *My Philosophical Development*. London: George Allen & Unwin.

Schmitt, Frederick. 1995. *Truth: A Primer*. Boulder, CO: Westview Press.

Searle, John. 1995. 1980, "Minds, Brains and Programs" *Behavioral and Brain Sciences*, Vol. 3, pp. 417–457.

———. 1995. *The Social Construction of Reality*. New York: Free Press.

———. 2002. "The Problem of Consciousness" in *Consciousness and Language*. Edited by John Searle. Cambridge: Cambridge University Press, pp. 7–17.

Spinoza, Baruch. 1992. *The Ethics*, Translated by Samuel Shirley, Edited by Seymour Feldman. Indianapolis: Hackett.

Suarez, Francisco. 1960. *Disputaciones Metafisicas*, Vol. II, Translated by Sergio Rabade Romeo, Salvador Caballero Sanchez, and Antonio Puigcerver Zanon. Madrid: Bibliotecha Hispanica De Filosofia.

Swoyer, Chris. 1982. "True For" in *Relativism, Cognitive and Moral*. Edited by .Jack W. Meiland and Michael Krausz. Notre Dame: University of Notre Dame Press.

Talbot, Brian. 2012. "Student Relativism: How I Learned to Stop Worrying and Love the Bomb" *Teaching Philosophy*, Vol. 35, No. 2, pp. 171–187.

Thagard, Paul. 2012. "Coherence: The Price is Right" *The Southern Journal of Philosophy*, Vol. 50, No. 1, pp. 42–49.

Thayer, H.S. 1982. *Pragmatism: The Classic Writings*. Indianapolis: Hackett.

Vision, Gerald. 2004. *Veritas*. Boston: MIT Press.

Walker, Ralph C.S. 1989. *The Coherence Theory of Truth*. London: Routledge.

Willard, Dallas. 1973. "The Absurdity of Thinking in Language" *Southwestern Journal of Philosophy*, Vol. IV, pp. 125–132.

———. 1979. "Husserl's Critique of Extenstionalist Logic: 'A logic that does not understand itself'" *Idealistic Studies*, Vol. 9, No. 2, pp. 142–164.

———. 1984. *Logic and the Objectivity of Knowledge*. Athens, OH: Ohio University Press, 1984.

————. 1991. "Toward a Phenomenology for the Correspondence Theory of Truth" appears in Italian as "Verso una teoria fenomenologica della verita come corrispondenza" *Discipline Filosofiche*, Vol. I, pp. 125–147.

————. 1993. "Predication as Originary Violence: A Phenomenological Critique of Derrida's View of Intentionality" in *Working Through Derrida*. Edited by G.B. Madison. Evanston, IL: Northwestern University Press.

————. 1999a. "How Concepts Relate the Mind to Its Objects" *Philosophia Christi*, Vol. 2, pp. 5–20.

————. 1999b. "Truth: Can We Do Without It?" *Christian Ethics Today*, Vol. 5, No. 2, pp. 12–15.

Wittgenstein, Ludwig. 1961. *Tractatus Logico-Philosophicus*, Translated by D.F. Pears and B.F. McGuinness. London: Routledge and Kegan Paul.

Yong, Sun and Haack, Susan. 2010. *Pragmatism Then and Now*, http://www.pragmatismtoday.eu/winter2010/Haack_Interview.pdf

Young, James. 2008. "The Coherence Theory of Truth" *The Stanford Encyclopedia of Philosophy*, Fall 2008, Edited by Edward N. Zalta, http://plato.stanford.edu/archives/fall2008/entries/truth-coherence/

Index

Note: Locators followed by the letter 'n' refer to notes.